# Gentle Hammer
# Friendly Sword
# Silent Arrow

## Other Publications by Madhukar Thompson:

### Books

- Enlightenment: An Outbreak
- Enlightenment May Or May Not Happen
- Enlightenment? Who Cares!
- Teachings en Route to Freedom*
- Enlightenment: Never Found — Never Lost*

### Postcard Books

(Sets of cards taking a light-hearted look at different aspects of spirituality and the search for Truth)

- Enlightenment by Airmail
- Enlightenment à la Carte
- Zorba 'n Buddha Your Way to Freedom*
- Of Jewels, Pigs and Freedom*
- The Seeker and His Search*
- Meditation*
- Enlightenment*
- Master!*

---

*Publication scheduled for December 1999

# Gentle Hammer
# Friendly Sword
# Silent Arrow

*An Introduction to the
Teachings of Ramesh S. Balsekar*

Edited by
Madhukar Thompson

Copyright © 1999 by
Madhukar Thompson


Published in India by

NETI NETI PRESS

8 Sheetal Apts.
Kawedewadi - Koregaon Park
P. O. Box 194
Pune 411001, India
Tel./Fax: (91-20) 603338; 6050020
e-mail: neti_neti@yahoo.com
www.neti-neti.org


Printed by:

SANGAM PRESS
17/B, Kothrud, Pune 411029, India


ISBN 0-9665245-3-5

*Dedicated to Ramesh S. Balsekar*

Enlightenment is an impersonal event. Because it is destined, no power on earth can hinder or enhance its occurrence.

—Ramesh S. Balsekar

# Contents

# Part 1
# Gentle Hammer

A Collection of Aphorisms Drawn from the Teachings
of Ramesh S. Balsekar

# Part 2
# Friendly Sword

Ramesh S. Balsekar Answers 24 Key Questions

# Part 3
# Silent Arrow

*The Search for God-Truth-Reality;* Article by Ramesh S. Balsekar published in "The Mountain Path," December 1991

Ramesh Balsekar with the Editor at Kovalam Beach

## Biographical Notes on Ramesh S. Balsekar and Madhukar Thompson

**Ramesh S. Balsekar** was born into a devout Hindu *brahmin* family in Bombay, on May 25, 1917. After his studies at the London School of Economics, he joined the Bank of India in 1940. He rose to become the bank's General Manager, and retired after thirty-seven years of service. Sri Balsekar married Sharda in 1940, and they raised three children.

Although Sri Ramana Maharshi (whom he never met in person) was one of his most important spiritual mentors, his personal guru for more than twenty years was Sri Vithal Rao Joshi who lived in Pune, a city some 180 kms south-east of Bombay. Sri Balsekar met his second and final guru—Sri Nisargadatta Maharaj—in Bombay in 1978. One year later, during *Diwali* (the Hindu "festival of lights"), Sri Balsekar attained enlightenment in Maharaj's presence. On September 6, 1981, Maharaj passed away, and Sri Balsekar began teaching in his own right. Since 1987 he has taught at public seminars held in Europe, the USA and India. He has also written ten books on the teachings of *Advaita* Vedanta.

Sri Balsekar meets seekers and answers their questions every morning from 10:00 a.m. to 11.30 a.m. at his residence in Bombay (Mumbai). During the last half-hour of these sessions, devotional songs (*bhajans*) are sung in his presence. Sri Balsekar's address is: Gamadia Road—Sindhula Bldg. (off Warden Road, near the French Consulate), Mumbai 400 026 (tel. 91-22-4927725). Sri Balsekar is affectionately known as "Ramesh," and is addressed thus by his devotees and other visiting seekers.

**Madhukar Thompson** first met Ramesh S. Balsekar on July 7, 1993 in Bombay. Besides attending his seminars in Kovalam Beach, Kerala, India in 1994 and 1995, he visited him perhaps a dozen times over the next two years. In August 1995, he settled in Bombay so as to be able to attend Ramesh's talks on a daily basis. Six months later, having come to an understanding of Ramesh's teachings, Madhukar moved to Pune, a city some 180 kilometers south-east of Bombay. He spends his time writing about *Advaita* Vedanta and his experiences with the numerous gurus and spiritual masters he met in the course of his search for enlightenment.

# Introduction

The average person mistakenly believes he is an individual entity that is separate from the totality of manifestation. He believes he has free will and personal volition; and he believes he is the body-mind organism that he owns, uses, enjoys and controls. Furthermore, he believes that his own efforts and doings will somehow suffice to bring him what he wants—including lasting happiness. However, sooner or later, his own life experiences will show him clearly that this belief is false. He will find that nothing he can do or acquire can bring him the peace he so desires.

Realizing this, his mind turns inwards. Now he will try to find lasting peace and happiness within. His spiritual search has begun. He has become a seeker. Now he may want to know more about the riddle of life, its purpose, and its end, the mystery and "reality" of the Creator (and who created the Creator, if there is one) and then perhaps the final and ultimate Reality beyond the Creator. He may begin to wonder "Who or what am I?", "What remains after death?", and he may keep asking other such existential and metaphysical questions and longing for answers to them. His search will not end until he has realized, through his own direct experience, who he really is. Only in this realization will he find lasting, final and complete peace, contentment and fulfillment—enlightenment.

Ramesh states that the seeking begins with an individual who is convinced that enlightenment is attainable through his personal efforts. The desire for freedom compels this individual to follow certain spiritual practices (*sadhanas*) in the belief that "Enlightenment must happen!" as a result. Underlying such pursuits is the conviction that if he only tries hard enough, he will be rewarded with lasting peace and happiness. Ramesh, however, teaches that the seeker —as an individual with personal volition and doership—just doesn't exist, hence there is nothing anyone can do to hasten his spiritual progress. It is God or Consciousness that turned the person into a seeker in the first place, and it is God or Consciousness that does the seeking and that recognizes Its own nature in the event of enlightenment.

According to Ramesh, the spiritual search is actually a process of disidentification "in which the apparently separate 'me'-entity, with the sense of individual free will and personal doership, gradually weakens until its final and total dissolution is reached." It is therefore impossible for the individual seeker to "make" progress happen; the process of dis-identification can only be witnessed. During this process, the seeker's progress can be "measured" by his attitude towards the spiritual search and enlightenment. The further the process advances the greater is the seeker's lack of concern about progress and enlightenment. The disidentification process nears completion when the seeker realizes that "Enlighten-ment may or may not happen." At this point he has finally and totally understood that he doesn't exist as an entity with personal will and doership. He therefore has no power to influence the outcome of his search; the occurrence of enlightenment depends strictly and entirely on God's Will alone.

As a result of this understanding, the attitude "Enlightenment? Who cares!" may then arise in the seeker, and this is seen by Ramesh as indicative of the imminent occurrence of enlightenment. At this stage, even the goal of enlightenment has lost its allure. The seeker understands that he has all the while been seeking enlightenment because he was hoping to enjoy it. Now he realizes that enlightenment (representing, as it does, the annihilation of the individual) is a state in which there will be no "enjoyer" left to delight in the culmination of the spiritual search, hence there is really no point getting all worked up about it—why bother? In short, the "hallmark" attitudes for the three stages of the disidentification process that leads to enlightenment, are:

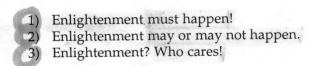

1) Enlightenment must happen!
2) Enlightenment may or may not happen.
3) Enlightenment? Who cares!

This book is intended to provide you, the reader, with some indication as to where you are at on the spiritual path, clarifying your own spiritual understanding and facilitating an honest appraisal of your situation. As you read on, one of the above attitudes (or hopefully enlightenment itself!) may resound and arise from the depth of your being, finding its echo and manifestation in your daily life.

The book may also raise new questions for you, leading on to further and deeper inquiry. It may make you aware that you need further guidance. If this is the case, you can always pay a visit to Ramesh in Bombay. I am sure he will welcome you cordially, greeting you along these lines: "You have come for the first time. What can I do for you? Tell me, what is your understanding!" He may say, "This teaching is a self-destructive process as far as the ego is concerned. Merely hearing it may bring about the understanding...," and he will willingly answer those questions which have driven you to his door.

Don't worry, though; you will not find Ramesh waiting for you in the garb of an armed samurai as depicted on the cover of this book. But you can be sure that he acts like a sumurai in the service of Truth, using his three "weapons," each of which is embodied in one of the chapters that follow. *Gentle Hammer* consists of 933 aphorisms drawn from his teachings, *Friendly Sword* conveys his teaching through a series of questions and answers, while in *Silent Arrow* the words flow out straight from Ramesh's own pen and heart.

After the persistent slogan-like hammering of the teaching, and the surgical excision of what is unreal from what is real, the final target—Understanding in and as the Heart—remains for the silent arrow of Ramesh's own writing to penetrate in the concluding part of the book. The book as a whole conveys Ramesh's compassionate and gentle teaching style, and his unique ability to adapt the ancient *Advaita* Vedanta teachings to suit the predicament of the modern-day seeker. The master uses his weapons skillfully and with utmost precision until—sooner or later—the annihilation of the ego is completed.

# Part 1

# Gentle Hammer

A Collection of Aphorisms Drawn from
the Teachings of  Ramesh S. Balsekar

*Satsang* in Ramesh's living Room; January 1996

Nikos: *The guru tells the seeker the real situation. And even though the seeker listens to the guru's words and understands them intellectually, he can't yet grasp the truth existentially. And what is worse, he can't do anything about it on his own account.*

Ramesh: And the guru repeats himself a thousand times. I'll tell you a story. During one of my seminars in the States, I was taken to a restaurant which had a dish called "Baked Potato in Clay." When it is served, the waiter carries along a tiny hammer and, in front of you, he keeps tapping the clay shell gently until the clay breaks, and the potato is there for you to eat. That's what this teaching does: gently hammering at the clay. That's why I call this teaching a self-destructive process. The constant hammering of the teaching destroys the identification of Consciousness with the particular body-mind organism. (*Excerpt from one of Ramesh's morning talks*)

# Introductory Note

*Gentle Hammer* features a series of 933 aphorisms which emerged from Ramesh's daily teaching sessions over a period of seven months (August 1995—March 1996). Each aphorism sums up one element of Ramesh's teaching and, taken together, they provide an overview of its main themes.

The aphorisms have been grouped together under various subject headings. For the sake of clarity, cross-references between major subject areas have been added so as to enable the reader to easily investigate a given theme and gain a deeper understanding of issues which are of particular interest.

The aphorisms' strength lies in their brevity and simplicity. They are like gentle but persistent hammer blows, tapping away at our egos and illusions. Relentless and often breathtakingly unexpected, the hammer blows rain down on our consciousness from all angles, shattering our old beliefs, misconceptions and wrong notions about the spiritual search and enlightenment, and about who or what we are.

Each time one of these hammer blow hits its target—the reader's Heart—the resulting understanding is immediate and direct beyond the intellect. And when a hammer blow misses its target—i.e. when the teaching it expresses is not understood as one's own existential actuality—it still fulfils a useful function by sharpening the reader's faculty of discernment and initiating a further process of inquiry. For the aphorisms are not necessarily meant to provide final answers; rather, they are intended to deepen and crystallize the reader's understanding, inspiring his spiritual search and keeping it keen until the ultimate recognition of his true nature occurs.

## 1. Acceptance

**(*See* All there is, is Consciousness; Being; Destiny; Free Will vs God's Will; What-Is)**

1. In the acceptance of What-is here/now there is no bondage and no freedom.
2. If you accept What-is, there is no need for the Supreme Power, or for any questions and answers about It.
3. Acceptance of the words "Thy Will be done" is the only formula in life to hang on to.
4. If you accept success or failure as destined, you will have no pride and no guilt.
5. By accepting "Thy Will be done," you surrender your individuality and free will to God.
6. Acceptance means the absence of personal will and doership.
7. The final acceptance is acceptance of the ego.
8. While listening to the teaching, there may be a moment in which it is accepted. That moment of acceptance is not a concept.
9. The acceptance of What-is is the sense of presence, the "I-Am."
10. Enlightenment may not happen. The acceptance or non-acceptance of this possibility will occur as destined.
11. The acceptance of life as it unfolds results in a mysterious spiritual alchemy: tolerance and generosity.

12. Acceptance is the only higher consciousness.
13. An accepting person is a conscious person.
14. Acceptance and non-acceptance are made of the same stuff—in heaven, by God.

## 2. Action

**(*See* Decision; Destiny; Free Will vs God's Will; *Karma*; Thought)**

1. No action is "my" action. All actions are God's actions.
2. Who is the saint and who is the sinner? All actions are God's actions.
3. Good and bad actions don't belong to the respective individuals: they are God's function.
4. There is no such thing as appropriate or inappropriate action; there is only action.
5. Trying to be passive is still an activity.
6. Plan whatever you think you want to do. But remember that your actions and their results are what God wants to happen.
7. Do what you can as well as you can, and then leave the consequences up to God.
8. What you will do in the future is still God's Will.
9. Act as if you have free will. But understand that, in fact, how you act is not in your hands, nor are the consequences of your action.
10. Intention has nothing to do with what actually comes to happen.

11. Every action, deed or event is part of the functioning of Totality and the Will of God.

12. To understand that every action is God's action, is to stand on high ground.

13. We cannot ask God, "Why are You doing what You are doing?"

14. A seeker's choice or action is always concerned with its outcome. A sage's choice or action is not concerned with its outcome.

15. Jesus says, "You will reap the fruits of your actions." Who will reap the fruits? The body-mind organism, not you.

16. What you consider to be "your" action actually occurs like this: God creates billions of body-mind organisms, which rather like computers, are programmed at the moment of conception via DNA and environmental conditioning. At a given time, He sends an outside impulse or input in the form of a thought or an event that is perceptible to one of the senses of the body-mind organism. The brain of the body-mind organism (like the hard drive of a computer) reacts to this outside impulse. It processes the input according to its programming (the DNA and environmental conditioning) and produces what you call "your" action as an output.

17. Action is reaction.

18. Your deeds are nothing but the reactions of your brain to something that is sensed.

19. It is not possible for there to be total action and total

awareness at the same time.
20. There is no causation. The effect needs the cause—
they are one event.

## 3. *Advaita* Vedanta

1. Vedanta is the study of the mechanics of phenomenality. The conclusion drawn from these studies is that there is no purpose or meaning in what happens.
2. The *bhakta* wants duality. However, the basis of *bhakti* and *jnana* is non-duality, oneness, *Advaita*.
3. The *Advaita* teaching is not for the ordinay person.

## 4. All there is, is Consciousness

### (*See* Being; God; What-Is)

1. All there is, is Consciousness, God, Totality the Source.
2. How can Consciousness know itself, if all there is, is Consciousness?
3. There has never been any separation; Subjectivity cannot be aware of the subject.
4. Consciousness cannot know Consciousness. Consciousness can only *be* Consciousness.
5. Pure Subjectivity cannot be understood, seen, felt, or experienced.

6. Consciousness cannot be an object of the mind.
7. Consciousness-in-action is God-in-action.
8. Consciousness-in-action is phenomenality.
9. Consciousness-in-action is energy.
10. We don't know what electricity is. But we know how it functions. The same is true with Consciousness. We don't know what it is. But we know how it functions: as phenomenality and as the sense of being.
11. Consciousness does not get into the body. The body is part of the manifestation created by Consciousness.
12. It is the same Consciousness functioning through the senses of every sentient being.
13. The body-mind organism and its senses sensing an object of sensing—all are Consciousness. All there is, is Consciousness.
14. The Knower, the impersonal Consciousness, is the same in Andy, Chuck, Carol and Jean.
15. There is no comprehender: all there is, is Consciousness.
16. Question: Do all things have consciousness? Answer: Consciousness has all things! All there is, is Consciousness.
17. When It identifies Itself with a "me" with personal will and doership, pure Consciousness becomes occluded.
18. Consciousness-in-action becomes understanding. Understanding-in-action becomes witnessing.

19. Consciousness can never die because it was never created.

## 5. Animal

1. The animal has the same sense of presence as the human being. The latter has the sense of presence plus mind-intellect.
2. The animal lives life as it comes; it wants neither happiness nor unhappiness; for it, food is happiness, and the stick is unhappiness.
3. The animal's life consists of "run or kill."
4. The animal is in permanent meditation. It has no thinking mind.
5. Question: Are animals enlightened? Answer: The animal has no concept of bondage and therefore no concept of enlightenment.

## 6. Being

**(*See* Acceptance; All there is, is Consciousness; Concepts; What-Is)**

1. You are not the body-mind organism. You are the impersonal Consciousness. All there is, is Consciousness.
2. All there is, is Consciousness. You can only be It.
3. Consciousness doesn't need to be told, "Be yourself!" Consciousness cannot help but be. All there is, is Consciousness. Being is Consciousness.

4. Who is told to "Be yourself?" Since "you" are just a concept, you cannot be told to do anything!

5. Often Maharaj used to say: "Just be!" "Just be!" means let the body-mind organism not keep thinking about itself.

   "Just be!" means let the body-mind organism not keep asking questions.

   "Just be!" means let the body-mind organism merely accept that whatever happens is the Will of God, functioning through the body-mind organism.

   "Just be!" means acceptance, surrender, and understanding that all there is, is Consciousness or God.

   "Just be!" means there is no "one" to be told to be. The being happens. The awareness of being, of existing, is Consciousness. There is no one to be.

6. Maharaj says, "Be in the beingness!" and you ask, "How can I be in the beingness when I am working?" Answer: "You are in the beingness when you are not horizontally involved in thinking."

7. "Just being" happens when the thinking mind is not there.

8. There cannot be any dispute about the awareness "I am, I exist." If you did not exist, you would not be able to debate whether or not you actually exist.

9. The sense "I am, I exist" is not born out of the mind.

10. "Being" is not in time and space.

11. To know God is to be God. In being God, there is no subject/object relationship. The God state thus

33

corresponds to the state of deep sleep.
12. "Being one with God" is an empty formula.

## 7. Body-Mind Organism

### (*See* Destiny; Manifestation; Programming)

1. All body-mind organisms are part of Consciousness.
2. The body-mind organism is one object in the totality of objects.
3. The body-mind organism is merely an instrument, endowed with the dubious gift of mind-intellect, which plays its part in the mechanics of phenomenality or Totality.
4. There is no awareness without a body-mind organism. The body-mind organism and awareness appear together.
5. It is the electricity that produces light, not the lamp. But electricity can only function as light if the lamp exists. In the same way, Consciousness can only function once sentient and insentient beings have appeared.
6. Question: Can I learn from the body? Answer: Who can learn what? There is no learner. And the body is merely a body-mind organism with a certain DNA and conditioning.
7. Hitler didn't exist. Hitler was merely a name given by his parents to a particular body-mind organism.
8. It is God who is sinning through the body-mind

organism that is labeled "sinner."

9. God created a body-mind organism called Hitler who, as part of the functioning of Totality, annihilated millions of Jews.

10. The psychopath Hitler and the saint Mother Teresa are both instruments created by God.

11. What exists is a body-mind organism—the person is merely a concept.

12. "Be totally convinced that you are merely an instrument operated upon by God and then do whatever you like." (*Ramakrishna Paramahamsa*)

13. All body-mind organisms are robots, created, directed, and empowered by God.

## 8. Bondage and Freedom

### (*See* Enlightenment)

1. Prior to the appearance of manifestation, there is no bondage and no freedom.

2. The human being and its mind-intellect create the concepts of bondage and freedom.

3. The attachment of the mind to sense-experiences is bondage.

4. Expectations regarding the future are bondage.

5. Desire for happiness and aversion to pain are both expectations, and therefore bondage.

6. The expectation of happiness is the very bondage that you are striving to free yourself from.

7. Freedom is freedom from the thinking mind.
8. Freedom is knowing you were never the seeker.
9. If you feel freed, or bound, by the trust you feel for the guru, he has merely given you more bondage.

## 9. Buddha

1. "For me, Buddha's most significant teaching is this: 'Events happen, deeds are being done, but there is no individual doer thereof.'" (*Ramesh*)

## 10. Compassion

1. Compassion and anger arise as a reaction to a perception. They are impersonal events.
2. Why does the *jnani* teach? Compassion is the true reason.

## 11. Concept

### (*See* Being)

1. The human being creates a concept of a separate "me"-entity that thinks, "I can get what I want." And when this "me"-entity finds out that it can't, it creates the concept of a God who will help it to achieve what it cannot achieve on its own.

2. Anything which requires the mind for it to exist, is a concept.
3. In phenomenality, the only thing that is not a concept is the sense of presence, being, existing, being alive. The sense of being cannot be disputed.
4. The sense of presence becomes a concept in terms of the unmanifest "I-I," because both the body-mind organism and the sense of presence are part of phenomenality.
5. Every concept is a concept in phenomenality.
6. "What comes from the mind?"—Concepts.
7. A concept is a vocalized thought.
8. Every "what if" is a concept of the thinking mind.
9. The nature of the human mind is to have concepts.
10. Once you accept the teaching that, "There is no 'me,'" you don't need any other concept.
11. The final concept "Thy Will be done" removes all other concepts.
12. The idea of "being true to myself" is just words—it too is a concept.
13. "I am That," "All there is, is Consciousness," "Everything that happens is God's Will," are mere concepts.
14. One of the most helpful concepts is "Wait and see what happens."
15. All concepts are misconceptions.

## 12. Creation

### (*See* Manifestation)

1. "Who has created the world?"—Nobody. There is no "who." God is not a "who." God is a concept.
2. When the seeker asks, "Why are we created?" the Supreme Power is not supreme anymore.
3. "God creates and programs the body-mind organism. But then who is God?"—The creation and the Creator are one and the same.
4. God's creation includes everything. That's why you can sing hallelujah to the fish market.
5. Through the billions of body-mind organisms, Consciousness creates consciousness and manifestation.
6. On waking up and on falling asleep, the beginning and the end of the world occurs each day, in an instant, for the individual.
7. The manifestation arises or is created when you wake up. To that extent, it is you who create the manifestation.

## 13. Death

1. Consciousness is pure Consciousness only at death.
2. In death, Consciousness cannot be aware of Itself because no subject/object division exists. In death, Consciousness is one.

3. What happens at death? That which you had limited to your own manifest body-mind organism returns to the unlimited unmanifest.
4. Death means death of the conceptual entity "me."
5. Death means death of the concepts of bondage and freedom.
6. You are born with nothing and you will die with nothing.
7. Perfection for the human being is not to exist.
8. You wake up from the personal dream into the living dream of manifestation. But the real waking up happens when you wake up into physical death.
9. Death is not enlightenment. In deep sleep, you go into death, but not into enlightenment.
10. The sage's death has nothing to do with enlightenment but with his destiny.
11. In death, the enlightened one and the ordinary person are the same.
12. Nobody is afraid of deep sleep, but everybody is afraid of death. However, they are exactly the same.
13. "Is life after death bliss?"—Find out who wants to know! That will be better than any answer!

## 14. Decision

### (*See* Action; Destiny; Free Will vs God's Will)

1. "How to make decisions?"—"You" cannot decide anything.

3. A decision is made by the intellect based on its experience.
2. The seeker asks, "Who decides?" The sage answers: "Who wants to know?"
4. Manfred thinks he is making a decision but, in fact, it is God who is making the decision.
5. No matter what you have decided, or what you are deciding, or what you will ever decide, what happens is what would have happened anyway according to God's Will.
6. Make a decision or toss a coin—what will happen is destined anyway.
7. The conversion of your decision into action is not up to you and your will; it is up to God.
8. Not to make a decision is still making a decision.
9. Waiting to see what happens is also a decision.
10. If you are hungry and you have no money, you cannot not make a decision. You will beg, steal, or do something, or die.
11. The sage neither accepts nor rejects anything. Although there is choice and decision in his case, he is not concerned with any of the consequences which result.
12. After you have understood "Thy Will be done," make decisions as if you have free will, knowing full well that the consequences of your decisions are not in your hands.

## 15. Deep Sleep State

### (*See* Dream State; "I-I"; Waking State)

1. There is no manifestation if everybody is dead or asleep.
2. In deep sleep, you are God.
3. Deep sleep is the same as death. Each person dies at night and is reborn the next morning.
4. Deep sleep is the representative of death.
5. In deep sleep, something is awake but this something is not Andy.
6. Madhukar is not present in deep sleep. But something is present—Consciousness.
7. In deep sleep and in the waking state, the same impersonal Awareness exists.
8. You have to *be* deep sleep to *know* it. But you cannot know it while you are it.
9. In deep sleep, consciousness is dormant.
10. Deep sleep cannot be experienced. However, it is the memory that supplies the information that good or bad sleep has occurred.
11. During deep sleep and meditation, the "me" is in suspension; however, like a bird in the nest, it is still alive.
12. In deep sleep, coma, and anesthesia, the "me" is absent.
13. "You" are not asleep, "you" are not awake—the body-mind organism is.

14. There is no awareness of deep sleep because "you" don't exist in deep sleep.
15. Sleeping and waking are truly not in your control.
16. In deep sleep and death, there is no difference between the sage and the non-sage.
17. Sleeping and waking up are beyond your will.
18. Neither a sage nor a non-sage can be aware of being awake or asleep during deep sleep.
19. It is merely make-believe for a sage to claim he is aware in deep sleep and in death.
20. In deep sleep, there is no question about enlightenment, and no desire for it.
21. The ordinary person is enlightened in deep sleep.

## 16. Desire

### (*See* Detachment)

1. Who desires? The body-mind organism which is programmed by the DNA and the environmental conditioning. Therefore, God is behind every desire, not a person.
2. Desire is based on the programming of the body-mind-organism. According to the programming, the desire may be wanting to live near the sea. But the destiny may be to live in the mountains.
3. How to fight a desire?—A desire is an impersonal event that happens according to the programming of the body-mind organism. The brain cannot

produce a desire or fight against one.

4. One has no responsibility for one's desires.
5. One's desire may be to be lazy. But one's destiny may be to work very hard.
6. Desire is the usurpation of God's Subjectivity by the ego, the "me."
7. Desire and expectation are the involvement of the thinking mind with the future.
8. The desire for enlightenment is the worst drug of all.
9. The desire for the experience of oneness is an obstruction to enlightenment.
10. The stronger the desire for enlightenment, the smaller the possibility of enlightenment occurring.
11. Freedom is freedom from desire for enlightenment.
12. Without desire and expectations, life unfolds here-now as it is—as the What-is.

## 17. Destiny and Predestination

**(See Action; Decision; Free Will vs God's Will; What-Is)**

1. Destiny is a concept in phenomenality.
2. The concept of destiny is derived from the concept "Thy Will be done."
3. Destiny equates to the Will of God.
4. The human being is a robot that is remote-controlled by God. What it does is destined.
5. In the *Bhagavad Gita*, Krishna tells Arjuna, the

individual, "All is destined. Whether you fight or not, and whom you fight, is not in your hands, nor if you win or loose. What happens is in God's hands and is destined."

6. All thinking, doing, seeking, and experiencing is destined.

7. Your destiny is set in stone.

8. Destiny cannot be changed.

9. Destiny is unknown. Even a change in destiny is destined.

10. What can be changed cannot be destiny. If an astrologer tells you what is going to happen and it doesn't happen, that doesn't mean destiny has changed. It means the astrologer was wrong in his prediction.

11. Everything happens exactly as it is supposed to happen, because such is destiny.

12. There is no way out of what is going to happen because everything is destined.

13. If you think the understanding "Thy Will be done" may be used as an excuse to act antisocially, remember that too is so destined.

14. What you think you are doing to someone depends on the destiny of the other person.

15. What you see is destined and your brain merely reacts to it, as destined. Therefore, what you do cannot be called "your" action.

16. If "getting a lousy deal" is destined, how can you hope to secure a better deal? But, of course that hope

is also destined.

17. There is no murderer and no murder victim: murder is given and received through two body-mind organisms, because it is so destined.

18. Destiny refers to the body-mind organism, not to a "me"-entity or a soul.

19. What happens is destined. Therefore, life can be seen as simply a series of movements reversing into a ready-made future.

20. Destiny means that all that happens is already the past—before it actually happens in a present moment.

21. Enlightenment happens because it is destined.

## 18. Detachment

### (*See* Desire)

1. Being bored with life is not detachment.
2. Real detachment is detachment from the concept of detachment.
3. True detachment is not even wanting enlightenment.

## 19. *Dharma*

1. The flower's blooming is its *dharma;* where, if, when and how it blooms is its destiny.
2. Question: How can one recognize one's *dharma*?

Answer: Some do and others don't—and that is destined.

3. You can find out your *dharma*—your natural physical, mental, and temperamental characteristics—through an aptitude test.

4. Not following one's *dharma* means spiritual danger.

## 20. Dream State (Personal Dream)

### (*See* Deep Sleep State; Waking State)

1. Personal dreams just arise like thoughts—they come from "outside."

2. Dreams are psychological reactions to the actions of the waking dream.

3. Psychological reactions in the personal dream depend on the programming of the body-mind organism in the living dream.

4. The personal dream is based on the individual's memory of daily life in the waking state.

5. In a lucid dream, the dreamer is aware that he is dreaming and of what he is dreaming.

6. Lucid dreaming means witnessing what happens in the personal dream.

7. Enlightenment has nothing to do with lucid dreams.

8. As long as actions happen through the body-mind organism of a sage—as long as he is alive— psychological reactions are bound to appear as personal dreams.

9. Personal dreams are in duality and are unreal.

## 21. Ego and Doership

**(*See* Free Will vs God's Will; Identification; Individual;
*Maya*; "Me")**

1. Show me your ego!
2. You are the ego. The mind-intellect is the ego. "You" don't exist. You exist only as a programmed body-mind organism.
3. Some people say: "Fight the ego! Kill the ego! You must get rid of the ego!" What ego? You are the ego!
4. You cannot kill the ego. You are the ego. You are the entity that believes it is special and separate. You are the belief in an entity.
5. The more you fight the ego, the stronger it becomes.
6. Man may kill himself, but he can't destroy the ego, because the ego is a natural phenomenon like a tree. It cannot commit hara-kiri.
7. "Get rid of the ego!" is a stupid command.
8. Don't oppose the ego! Accept the ego—if you can.
9. The ego cannot get rid of the ego, it is Totality that does the job.
10. The ego disappears through understanding and not through any effort by an individual. The individual is the ego.
11. Healthy ego - unhealthy ego: the psychotherapist is an ego-plumber.

12. Events happen anyway, but the ego thinks it has done it all.
13. The ego is part of What-is. Oneness and separation are concepts. They exist only when the ego exists.

## 22. Enlightenment

**(*See* Bondage and Freedom)**

### Enlightenment

1. Enlightenment is destined not programmed.
2. Enlightenment means that the sense of personal doership disappears and the individual seeker is annihilated. And when the individual seeker is annihilated the seeking stops. Then, there is no seeker, no seeking and nothing to be sought.
3. Enlightenment is the constant awareness and understanding that whatever happens is part of the functioning of Totality and that there is no "me"-entity with a sense of personal doership.
4. Enlightenment is not something that is acquired; it occurs when the sense of personal doership is lost.
5. Enlightenment is the absence of the thinker, the doer, and the experiencer.
6. Enlightenment is the end of wanting.
7. The common factor in all enlightened beings is that seeking has stopped.
8. Enlightenment means the death of the seeker.

9. No individual can be an enlightened man or woman.
10. To call someone enlightened is a contradiction in terms. No "one" can be enlightened.
11. If somebody thinks he is enlightened, he is deluded.
12. The absence of personal doership, i.e. enlightenment, cannot be proved.
13. Enlightenment is known but there is no knower.
14. Enlightenment means accepting the fact that life is a *leela*.
15. Enlightenment is not an object or an experience.
16. "You" cannot be the experiencer and have the experience of enlightenment.
17. Sorry, enlightenment cannot be enjoyed.
18. Enlightenment is merely an event like an earthquake or a flood.
19. Enlightenment is not a thoughtless state.
20. Enlightenment is a concept that goes hand-in-hand with the concept of bondage.
21. Enlightenment means the abandonment of all concepts.
22. There is no such thing as enlightenment. Liberation means only the liberation from the concept of bondage.
23. Enlightenment brings about the peace of acceptance. But it is not a permanent blissful state.
24. Total acceptance of What-is, is enlightenment.
25. Enlightenment means witnessing and accepting everything as it is.
26. Enlightenment is not permanent happiness.

27. Enlightenment is the absence of involvement in happiness and unhappiness.
28. It is old-fashioned to believe that *siddhis* are a sign of enlightenment.
29. Omniscience and the ability to make accurate predictions are not part of the nature of enlightenment.
30. Deliverance is gradual, awakening is sudden.
31. Enlightenment has no meaning.
32. Every sage has a different concept of enlightenment.
33. Sai Baba used to say, "I will give you *moksha*." He is wrong. *He* can't give it.

## Obstructions to Enlightenment

1. Wanting enlightenment is an obstruction to enlightenment.
2. Question: What prevents enlightenment? Answer: The thinking mind wanting enlightenment.
3. Mental illness is the biggest obstacle for enlightenment.
4. The seeker's desire to hasten the process of enlightenment is an obstruction. However, this desire arises because it is God's Will.
5. Question: Is practice an enhancement or an obstacle to enlightenment? Answer: It can be both. Whatever it is, it is destined.
6. No power on earth can prevent enlightenment from happening if it is destined to happen. And no power

on earth can make enlightenment happen if it is destined not to happen.

## Enlightenment: May or May Not Happen

1. Enlightenment may or may not happen in this body-mind organism.
2. It takes tremendous courage to accept that enlightenment may not happen.
3. Enlightenment may or may not happen—you are stitched up. In the meantime you may entertain yourself by meditating or by watching soap operas.
4. After accepting that enlightenment may not happen, the ride of life may be enjoyed or suffered.
5. The penultimate state before enlightenment is: "I don't care even if I do care about enlightenment!"
6. If the understanding is "All there is, is God" then it doesn't matter if one is enlightened or not.
7. Enlightenment happens after accepting that it may not happen.

## Enlightenment: Before the Occurrence

1. Before enlightenment: No way.
2. Before and after enlightenment: No way back.
3. No person can achieve enlightenment.
4. Enlightenment is not an object to be achieved—it just happens.

5. Enlightenment happens when Consciousness wants it to happen.
6. Enlightenment can only happen if there is the deepest possible conviction that there is no individual to whom enlightenment can happen.
7. Question: Are there different levels of enlightenment? Answer: No. But there are different levels of understanding.
8. The experience of oneness is not a necessary condition for enlightenment to happen.
9. Enlightenment has no restrictions. It can occur to both a beggar and a millionaire.
10. "Who cares!" or, "It doesn't matter" are expressions of the penultimate understanding before enlightenment.

### Enlightenment: During the Occurrence

1. When enlightenment happens, one may exclaim, "It is so simple! It really doesn't matter!"
2. The event of enlightenment comes as a surprise for the individual because he had stopped seeking it long ago. Enlightenment can only happen after seeking has stopped. And the seeking stops only when the non-existence of the individual seeker is realized.
3. The occurrence of enlightenment is usually accompanied by emotions. They arise as a sort of

proof that the understanding has happened.

4. The actual experience of enlightenment does not happen to an individual.

## Enlightenment: After the Occurrence

1. After enlightenment there is no "me" and no "other," and no personal doership.
2. Enlightenment is automatically followed by right living.
3. Enlightenment initiates a change in attitude towards life but not a change in behavior.
4. After enlightenment, What-is is accepted as part of the impersonal functioning of Totality.
5. After enlightenment, all judging comes to an end.
6. Happiness and unhappiness continue after enlightenment.
7. "Does a constant and special awareness prevail after enlightenment?"—Yes, the constant awareness of no personal doership.
8. "Does enlightenment help the world?"—God does not need any help from anyone.

## Enlightenment and the Taoist

1. For the Taoist, the process of enlightenment passes through three stages or levels. On the first level, the rivers, mountains and the individual who perceives

them are assumed to be real. On the second level, the rivers and mountains are seen to be unreal, but this perception of unreality does not yet extend to the individual himself. The individual still perceives himself as having a very real and separate identity. On the third and final level, all sense of individuality and personal doership have vanished, and the rivers, mountains and the body-mind organism that perceives them are all recognized as being part of the unreal living dream. This living dream—the manifestation—is only real in as much as it appears. It is unreal because its appearance depends on its essence—Consciousness.

## 23. Evolution

1. Evolution occurs in phenomenality; Consciousness does not evolve. Consciousness was and will always be the same.
2. Evolution is *leela*.
3. Evolution occurs in phenomenality, i.e. in the personal dream and in the living dream.

## 24. Experience

1. An experience or an event merely happens through a body-mind organism. For an experience to happen, there is no need for any "one."

2. Every experience is impersonal; memory is personal.
3. Consciousness-at-rest cannot be experienced; all experiences can only be experienced by a body-mind organism.
4. It is Consciousness that experiences, through the body-mind organism, the highest ecstasy and the worst misery.
5. God cannot be experienced.
6. Consciousness is one. There is nothing for Consciousness to experience.
7. God has no need for a continuous feeling or experience of oneness and peace.
8. Every experience occurs in the realm of the mind. Reality is beyond the purview of the mind.
9. Experience has no importance. In *Advaita*, it is merely seen for what it is: a fleeting appearance.
10. Any experience that does not last forever is worth nothing.
11. What exists at all times cannot be called an experience.
12. Seeker: Is the experience of oneness, that happened to you (the sage) some years ago, permanently established? Sage: Permanently for "whom"? There cannot be any impersonal experience.
13. Experiences happen to the "me." No experience can continue without the "me."
14. The body-mind organism of the sage continues to function according to its programming. But there is no one there to experience an experience.

## 25. Faith and Trust

1. Faith is part of destiny. You are destined to have faith or not to have faith. But "faith" is just a word.
2. You claim to have trust in God and to have faith in Him, because you want Him to be kind to you.
3. "Trust in God" implies the hope that He will do what you want.
4. "I have faith in God" means, "I want to have a good relationship with God."
5. When life doesn't go according to your expectations, you lose faith. Often, life is losing faith.
6. Real trust in God occurs when you are in a mess.
7. The seeker says, "I don't want to lose faith."—Why should he not lose faith?
8. Trust in God really means, "Thy Will be done," in the absence of the "me" and personal will.

## 26. Free Will vs God's Will

(*See* Action; Decision; Destiny and Predestination; What-Is)

1. Many people want to hear this teaching, but only a few can actually come; that is because God has willed it so.
2. The final and most important question is: Is there such a thing as individual free will or does everything happen according to God's Will?

3. By accepting "Thy Will be done," you surrender your individuality and free will to God.

4. Birth and death are beyond one's choice, as are all life's events in between. They are all willed by God.

5. The sperm did not decide to be in the womb. How much less can you have chosen your parents—there is no "you."

6. *Ramakrishna Paramahamsa* says, "Be totally convinced that you are merely an instrument of God through which He acts, and then do whatever you like." *Ramesh* continues, "Act as if you have free will, but know that you are merely a body-mind organism created by God. Whatever happens through it is part of functioning of Totality and according to God's Will."

7. No power on earth can restrict the Will of God.

8. Asking "Why?" means restricting God's Will.

9. By complaining, "God is erratic, psychopathic, etc." you are hanging Him! You cannot restrict His Will with your judgements.

10. God's Will makes you think that you have your own personal will.

11. Man's reaction to an event is natural; the consequences of a reaction to an event are unlimited. Personal will is wanting to limit the unlimited possibilities, to confine them to what you want to happen. However, in both cases, the consequences depend entirely on God's Will.

12. "Thy Will be done" is the core of any true religion.

13. There is no room for your will if you accept that whatever happens is part of the functioning of Totality.

14. A cow tied to a pole by a rope has limited freedom. Not so the human being. God does not give even a rope's length of freedom to him. Whatever happens, happens according to His Will.

15. God does not share His Will with you.

16. Even what you intend to do is God's Will.

17. "What cannot be cured, must be endured" is the English proverb for "Thy Will be done."

18. There is no free will. Adam and Eve proved it. Although God told them, "Don't eat the apple!" they ate it anyway—because of His Will.

19. The victim cries out "Poor me!"—So what! What happened to you is the Will of God.

20. Whenever you say, "It so happened that..." you prove that you have no free will.

21. "Me" means free will.

22. "I" is arrogance. "My will" is arrogance.

23. Billions of separate "me's" believe in free will. And that is life as we know it. And that is God's Will.

24. The understanding "Thy Will be done" can produce either a sense of freedom from responsibility for one's actions, or a sense of helplessness: "I am nobody and I have no power and I have no purpose."

25. When you accept the non-existence of the "me," free will disappears and God's Will prevails.

26. As long as you believe in free will, enlightenment cannot happen
27. "Thy Will be done" can only be said if it is willed by God.
28. "Thy Will be done" does not mean, "Thy Will is not being done now." God's Will is *always* done now. All that happens is God's Will.
29. Will you blame God if you win the lottery?
30. "Thy Will be done" is a conversation stopper.
31. How to make God laugh? Tell him about your plans for the future.

## 27. God

### (*See* All there is, is Consciousness)

1. Because the human being cannot get what it wants, it creates the concept of God and prays to Him, "Give me this, don't give me that." .
2. The concept of a separate human entity necessitates the concept of God.
3. God is the personalized concept of the impersonal concept, the Supreme Power, Totality, Consciousness.
4. "What is God?"—That which you are not!
5. Other than God, nothing is.
6. Seeker: "What is God?" Sage: "Perfection." Seeker: "I want perfection."
7. The seeker's problem is that he wants to be God.
8. You cannot be God! To be God is a natural

impossibility—All there is, is God.

9. Who is to be God? God is all there is.

10. God is impersonalized Totality.

11. There is only God—total Subjectivity.

12. Subjectivity and objectivity cannot meet.

13. God is pure Subjectivity. Subjectivity has no object to enjoy.

14. God is the sole and only Subject. All sentient and insentient beings are its object.

15. The Source has no need to know itself.

16. God cannot *know* God. God can only *be* God.

17. God cannot know God other than through His creation.

18. God is the Supreme Hypnotist who makes most human beings believe they are separate entities.

19. "Does God have an intention?"—Who wants to know?

20. "Does God decide at random? Are religions made by God?"—Who wants to know?

21. "God should be all merciful and compassionate."— Why should He? Who told you that? God has no limitations.

22. "They say Satya Sai Baba is God."—How can Satya Sai Baba be God, if all there is, is God?

23. You want to know God?—Forget it!

## 28. Grace

1. "What is Grace?"—Grace is a description of the world.

2. God's Will is God's Grace—it is not always beautiful.

3. Grace is good and bad.
4. Misery is God's Grace too.
5. If God's Grace doesn't happen, that is still God's Grace.
6. God's Grace is God's Will and that is What-is.
7. The Grace that occurs in the presence of a guru is God's Grace.
8. In a moment of Grace, the manifest and the unmanifest are one.
9. "How does Grace work?"—Who wants to know?

## 29. Guru

1. The guru is a concept and part of phenomenality.
2. The guru's behavior and conduct are merely a concept held by the disciple (and by some gurus).
3. A guru is born when people come to a particular person with their practical and spiritual difficulties.
4. The guru is not beyond the law of Totality.
5. The guru is like the shining sun. Does the sun rise or set?
6. The guru's answers are God's answers.

## 30. Guru/Fake

1. Fake and genuine gurus are both part of the functioning of Totality.
2. The fake sage acquires a holy personality. The true

sage may drink, smoke or swear, but he has lost his personality.

3. The fake guru says, "Come unto me and I shall give you enlightenment."

4. It is arrogance for a guru to claim that he gives you anything.

5. Fake gurus take advantage of the seeker by making him give them money.

6. To judge the fake guru is to judge God.

7. There are three types of guru: a) gurus who are enlightened—they are genuine; b) gurus who think they are enlightened—they are sincere; and c) gurus who know they are not enlightened—they are fake.

8. Question: How can I check if a guru is genuine? Answer: If he doesn't think before he answers, if he answers spontaneously, he is genuine.

## 31. Guru-Disciple Relationship

1. Question: "How does the guru-disciple relationship come into existence?" Counter question: "How does the sun rise in the morning?"

2. The guru is like the sun. Being light, the sun knows neither darkness nor light.

3. The spiritual search is twofold: the search for the guru and the search for enlightenment. Finding the guru, half the job is done.

4. When the guru is found, it is his responsibility to

bring about the understanding in the seeker.

5. Finding the guru, the seeking goes on.

6. The seeker and the guru are one event. What will happen out of their meeting is up to God.

7. The guru and the disciple are not individuals. Therefore, who could teach what to whom?

8. The word guru includes all dualities: guru and disciple, truth and illusion, knowledge and ignorance, etc.

9. The only difference between the guru and the disciple is that one is playing the role of the guru and the other is playing the role of the disciple.

10. The guru and the disciple are like the river and the ocean. The river is only separate from the ocean until it reaches it.

11. The guru and the disciple are like camphor and fire; in coming together both eventually disappear.

12. The disciple and the guru dissolve in the final understanding: "All there is, is Consciousness.

13. Not every seeker who comes to the guru gets what he seeks.

14. The genuine guru can tell his disciple: "Go to any other guru you like."

15. Guru-hopping is not the seeker's sport or choice but his destiny.

16. Sitting in silence with the guru can be a way of passing the time, a spiritual practice or a teaching.

17. The presence of the guru does something for the seeker's spiritual advancement. What it does and

how it does this is not known.
18. The guru's presence brings about the guru's Grace.
19. The guru-disciple relationship is part of the phenomenal illusion.

## 32. Happiness

*(See* **Suffering**)

1. Bliss is an interpretation of a state.
2. Bliss is part of manifestation. It does not exist in deep sleep.
3. Unhappiness means things don't happen according to your expectations.
4. Seeking enlightenment is seeking happiness.
5. The human being and its mind-intellect create happiness and unhappiness.
6. No teaching can make you happier. Happiness and misery are part of destiny; no power on earth can change it.
7. The teaching does not produce more happiness or less misery; but it produces less judgement about what is supposed to be happiness or misery.
8. Happiness means no pride, no guilt, no enmity.
9. Helping others and making others happy is the formula that makes you yourself happy.
10. When work is worship, it becomes the key to happiness.
11. The acceptance of the teaching "Thy Will be done" brings about more happiness.

## 33. Identification

**(*See* Ego and Doership; Individual; *Maya;* "Me")**

1. *Maya* is the identification of the impersonal Consciousness with a body-mind organism, by means of which the personal doer is created.
2. Identification is part of the mechanics of phenomenality.
3. In the seeker, understanding and identification alternate.
4. For the sage, there is identification with the body-mind organism, but not as an individual doer.
5. Life means both the simultaneously ongoing processes of identification and disidentification proceeding through many lives.
6. Enlightenment does not mean disidentification with the body-mind organism. It means disidentification with the "me," the doer.

## 34. "I-I"—"I-Am"—"I am Andy"

**(*See* Deep Sleep State)**

### "I-I"

1. Potential impersonal energy: "I-I"—Consciousness-not-aware-of-itself.
   Manifested impersonal energy: "I-Am"—

Consciousness-aware-of-itself.
Identified personal energy: "I am Robert"—
Consciousness identifying itself with a body-mind organism.

2. The "I-I" is pure Subjectivity without the slightest trace of objectivity.

3. With the appearance of manifestation, the "I-I" becomes "I-Am," and the "I-I" is the manifestation. They are not two.

4. Prior to deep sleep, there is "I-I." In deep sleep, there is "I-Am" for the sage and the non-sage alike. In the personal dream, there is "I-Am" (for the sage) or "I am Robert" (for the non-sage). In the living dream, there is "I-Am" (for the sage) or "I am Robert" (for the non-sage). In a past-life experience, there is "I-Am" (for the sage) or "I am Robert" (for the non-sage).

5. "I-I," "I-Am," "I am Robert" are not three states— All there is, is Consciousness.

6. You cannot be in the "I-I" as long as you have a body.

## "I-Am"

1. "What is not born out of the mind?"—The source of the mind: Consciousness, the sense of "I-Am."

2. The feeling of "I-am, I exist, I am alive" is nothing other than God.

3. There is no "one" to be in the state of "I-Am." "I-Am" is impersonal Consciousness.

4. Apart from What-is and "I-Am" nothing can be gotten.
5. When there is no "me," the "I-Am" is.
6. *Aham*—I am—is the actual thoughtless "I-Am." *Aham* is not a concept.
7. When Andy disappears, the "I-Am" remains.
8. Seeker: Is the "I am-ness" experience permanent for the sage? Sage: "Whose" experience? For the sage there is no "me" to have any experience.
9. The child is the "I-Am" plus ignorance. The *jnani* is the "I-Am" plus knowledge.
10. Question: Does knowledge expand? Answer: The only real knowledge is "I-Am."

## "I am Andy"

1. "I am Andy" means trouble.
2. The personality of John is merely a product of genes and environmental conditioning.
3. Question: Who is the "That" in "I am That"? Answer: It is the "me" that is being told you are "That" (Consciousness). You are not the body-mind organism. All there is, is Consciousness.
4. Maharaj says: "Just Be!" I say, "You are either 'just being' or you are 'being Michael.'"
5. Before the idea "I am John" arises, there is no path, no goal, no free will, no predestination, no creation, no dissolution.

## 35. Individual

**(See Ego and Doership; Identification; *Maya*; "Me")**

1. The concept of a separate individual necessitates the concept of God.
2. The concept of the individual—the part— necessitates the concept of God—the Whole.
3. If there is no concept of an individual, there can be no concept of God.
4. The individual is merely a programmed body-mind organism with certain natural characteristics.
5. The personality of an individual is comprised of a set of genes laid down at conception and a set of environmental conditionings.
6. Individuality is the restriction of Consciousness to yourself.
7. The individual "Claire" thinks "others" are also individuals.
8. The individual is unreal and non-existent.
9. Love is the disappearance of the separate individual.

## 36. Judgement

**(See Thinking Mind vs Working Mind; Witnessing)**

1. "Who makes the judgement?"—The thinking mind.
2. You may think, "I must not judge!" But how can you avoid judging? You cannot make yourself not

judge simply by your will or efforts.

3. When the mind is observing, it is done by the individual "me"; therefore, there is judgement and comparison. When witnessing occurs it is impersonal; therefore, there is no judgement and no comparison.

4. Seeing a red rose and a white rose is witnessing, but "I like the red rose more than the white one" is judging.

5. To judge is to judge God.

6. Question: I don't want to be judged. How to live without getting judged? Answer: Understand that there is no "one" who lives.

## 37. *Karma*

### (*See* Action)

1. *Karma* is action.

2. *Karma* means action, not intention. The intention behind a decision to act doesn't influence *karma* because God produces all *karma*.

3. The theory of *karma* is correct: the cause leads to the effect. However, *karma* is produced by God and not by the individual.

4. Actions occur not because of your will, or because of any expected reward or punishment, or because of your past *karma*; they occur because they are destined by God.

5. For many, *karma* means hope. They think they have personal volition, and responsibility for their actions and their consequences.

6. *Karma* concerns the body-mind organism, not the soul.

### 38. Life

1. Life means that Consciousness or energy function impersonally through the programmed body-mind organism. The reactions of the brain to outside impulses—which are generated by the same Consciousness—produce actions.

2. A particular event concerns the individual body-mind organism and its reaction to that event. Life consists of the totality of events.

3. Life: God starts the novel of creation with certain actions, presents the consequences of those actions and lets the characters merely respond to their causes and effects.

4. Life means experiencing. Life means one's personal experience.

5. Your life is God's life.

6. God-in-action is the flow of life.

7. Life is a movie—but it's happening "live."

8. In life you get fired at point blank. You can't tell life, "Wait a minute!"

9. "What is the meaning of life?"—Go forth and multiply! Why not?

10. "What is the meaning in life?"—That it ends in death.

11. Who wants to know the meaning of life? Find out!

12. Life is God's play or *leela*; it has no purpose and meaning.

13. The meaning of life is that it has no meaning.

14. Life is a mixture of good and evil.

15. Life is a continuous play of opposites, the good and the bad.

16. Life is both fair and unfair.

17. "How does one live?"—One does not live. Living happens. There is no "one."

18. Question: Is life a learning process? Answer: "Who" is to learn?

19. The purpose of learning from life is to acquire something. But something for whom?

20. There is no purpose in learning from life. Even if you become a better individual through learning, you still remain an individual.

21. You can't learn how to live life, because you are being lived.

22. The therapist says to the client: "You are responsible for your life. Therefore you can change it." The guru says to the disciple: "You will undergo therapy, but your life will only change as a result, if it is so destined."

23. Life cannot be learned, but it can be accepted as it unfolds.

24. Life for most people involves a refusal to witness.

25. When you are with the flow of life, no questions arise. When you are against the flow of life, questions arise.

26. Acceptance of the words "Thy Will be done" is the only formula in life to hang on to.
27. The acceptance of life as it unfolds results in a mysterious spiritual alchemy: tolerance and generosity.
28. Because life is predestined, it is actually a past life.
29. Life's novel can only be known page by page.
30. Life occurs page by page; you can't skip any pages.
31. Life is like a bowl of spaghetti—it is one mass; you cannot separate the strands of its events from each other.
32. If life is a dream, birth and death cannot be real.

## 39. Manifestation

**(*See* Creation; Phenomenality)**

1. Before the Big Bang there is potential energy, or Consciousness-not-aware-of-itself.
2. Ramana Maharshi's "No creation, no dissolution, no path, no goal, no free will, no predestination" describes the state prior to manifestation. The deep-sleep state is the corresponding state in phenomenality.
3. With the Big Bang, Consciousness became aware of itself and created manifestation.
4. The manifestation is complete, ready-made by God.
5. This world is God's TV on which He can watch His play.

6. Existence is like a ten-mile-long painting of which you can see only a tiny part at any given time.

7. The ready-made picture of manifestation is a concept, a speculation.

8. Manifestation is one single object.

9. "Is the manifestation a self-generating process or is it ready-made?"—The real question is, "Is it Thy Will or my will that prevails?" If the answer is "my will," then all other concepts follow.

10. Consciousness is aware of manifestation only when the body-mind organism is alive and awake.

11. Nothing exists "out there." Objects exist only in your mind. Without mind and consciousness, objects cannot exist. The sage and the scientist both know this fact.

12. The Big Bang occurs at the beginning of both the personal dream and the living dream: in an instant, mountains and rivers, billions of years old, arise, babies are born and old people die.

13. The intellect joins all the many present moments together, making time.

14. Space/time is the mechanism through which manifestation can be perceived.

15. Without an observer there is no manifestation.

16. Manifestation, and the body-mind organism as part of it, have no reality of their own. They depend on the Essence, the Source—Consciousness.

17. The mechanics of phenomenality are irrelevant if you accept that phenomenality is not real.

## 40. *Maya*

**(*See* Identification; Individual; "Me"; Reality)**

1. *Maya* is the identification of the impersonal Consciousness with a body-mind organism through which the personal doer is created.
2. *Maya*—the Divine hypnosis—makes the individual think that he has free will and that he is an individual doer.
3. If 2,000 people can be hypnotized by a third-rate hypnotist, just imagine what the Supreme Power can do!
4. *Maya* makes you believe that you exist as a separate entity in manifestation, in this so-called "reality."
5. *Maya* makes Alain seem to be real, and to exist separate from What-is.
6. *Maya*, the Divine hypnosis, makes the human being believe that the body-mind organism and the manifestation are real.
7. "I am Jayanti" is *maya*; "I-Am" is neither *maya* nor a concept.
8. What does not exist at all times is unreal.
9. "Is this talk also *maya*?"—Yes!

## 41. "Me"

**(*See* Ego and Doership; Identification; Individual)**

1. As long as the concept of the "me" has not arisen,

there is no question of enlightenment.

2. The "I-thought," or the "me"-thought, is the beginning of all thinking.

3. "Who asks questions?"—The "me."

4. First the human mind creates the concepts of a "me" and God, and then it asks questions about them.

5. Alain is what he thinks he is.

6. You may have a Christian or a Sanskrit name—both mean attachment to, and identification with, the "me."

7. "I am concerned."—Who is concerned? It is the "me."

8. The answer to all spiritual questions is: "Why should you know? Who wants to know? And once you know it, what are you going to do with it?"

9. The main spiritual question is: Who wants to know? Answer: The "me."

10. The same "me" experiences the events in the personal dream, in the living dream and in a past-life experience.

11. Like a drug addict to drug experiences, so the "me," the seeker, becomes addicted to spiritual experiences.

12. When there is no "me," there is no experience.

13. "Sleeping while awake" means the absence of the sense of "me."

14. "God," "Consciousness," "Totality," or "Supreme Power" mean simply the absence of the "me."

15. Question: Is the "me" capable of understanding God's Will? Answer: You are a tiny screw among billions of nuts, bolts and screws in a big machine.

How could a tiny screw understand the workings of the big machine?

16. The "me" seeks Subjectivity. But no object can become the subject.

17. Individuality is the restriction of Consciousness to yourself.

18. When you say "I" ("me"), you have forgotten God.

19. The annihilation of the "me" is the meeting place of surrender (*bhakti*) and knowledge (*jnana*).

20. Once the sense of personal doership has been annihilated, live however you like.

21. The instruction "Do whatever you like" is not valued by the "me"—the seeker.

22. Because there is no "me" and no expectations after enlightenment, the What-is is accepted.

23. Not to know what "I" want is What-is.

24. The essential qualification for witnessing is no "me."

25. In the waking state, the "me" exists in the ordinary person but not in the sage. In deep sleep, there is no awareness and no "me" for either of them.

26. For the sage, the waking and the deep-sleep states are the same because there is no "me" in either state.

27. "Who is the 'me'?"—At some point the question will drop without finding an answer. Consciousness cannot understand an object. Consciousness is all there is.

28. "Who understands the teaching correctly or incorrectly? Who wants to get something out of the teaching?"—The "me."

29. In reply to any spiritual question, the counter-question "Who wants to know?" serves as the return-button, always leading you back to the basic understanding that there is no "you."
30. The "me," the individual, is unreal and non-existent.
31. Enlightenment does not mean disidentification with the body-mind organism. It means disidentification with the "me," the doer.

## 42. Meditation

### (See Practice)

1. Meditation is spiritual practice for the beginner.
2. Meditation is like tennis lessons: for beginners only.
3. Meditation is preparing the body-mind organism for its programming to operate.
4. No matter what the results are, you must meditate if it so destined.
5. It's alright to meditate. But expecting results from meditation is an obstruction to enlightenment.
6. If you have no goal, meditation is wonderful.
7. Thoughts occur to the individual meditator.
8. For a seeker, meditation usually means an "I" having thoughts or not. But you cannot control the arising or dissolving of thoughts.
9. In true meditation, there is no thinking mind. However, you may sit in meditation for a million years,

and still the arising of a thought cannot be prevented.

10. "More awareness—less thoughts" is the wrong formula for meditation.

11. Meditation and practice cannot produce states of less or no thought or of more witnessing.

12. Four hours of meditation is considered superior to one hour's meditation—superior, that is, for the "me."

13. Less thoughts and more silence are not caused by meditation.

14. Thoughts being witnessed—but not by a "me"—is true meditation.

15. Total concentration on your work is meditation.

16. Meditation in daily life means witnessing whatever happens as the Will of God.

17. In true meditation, the "me" has disappeared.

18. In true meditation, there is no "me," no individual meditator, no goal, no enlightenment.

19. In true meditation, even the sense of presence disappears.

20. True meditation is something like deep sleep. In true meditation manifestation is not present.

## 43. Mind

**(See Thinking Mind vs Working Mind; Thought and Memory)**

1. First the mind creates questions and then it demands the answers.

2. The mind is nothing but a series of involved thinking spells.
3. Mind or ego cannot develop. They are part of the programming.
4. Mind is in time.
5. Meaning is the curse of the mind.
6. The mind is continuous—and you are only 25!
7. The human mind cannot understand the What-is.
8. The human mind cannot know the working of the Supreme Power.
9. The human mind cannot understand pure Subjectivity.
10. You talk about going beyond mind. Who is going beyond mind?
11. "Purity of the mind" is part of the impersonal functioning of Totality.
12. The inner voice is the mind.

## 44. Murder, Murderer, Murdered

1. Wars and murders are God's Will.
2. The murder, the murderer, and the murdered are one impersonal event.
3. The murderer is free of responsibility because it is God who has murdered through a body-mind organism. The possible consequent punishment again happens to a body-mind organism, not to an individual.

4.  The body-mind organism murders and gets punished, not "you."
5.  A murder can be committed even through the body-mind organism of an enlightened sage.

## 45. Past Life, Reincarnation and Rebirth

1.  A past-life experience is a personal dream based on memories of a previous life.
2.  A past-life experience is a personal dream in the waking state.
3.  A past life is an experience in somebody's life. That's all.
4.  Rebirth, reincarnation and past lives are part of the mechanics of the manifestation.
5.  Good and bad deeds direct the journey of the reincarnating soul—which doesn't exist.
6.  The seeker's spiritual capital derives from thousands of earlier body-mind organisms. It comes from the pool of Consciousness
7.  Mozart and Ramana Maharshi are the fruition of many lives.
8.  Enlightenment does not occur to all 10,000 past-life organisms, because they are not connected through a common soul.
9.  A past life is a concept.

## 46. Path

**(*See* Enlightenment; Practice; Process and Progress)**

1. "Is there a path?"—A path for whom?
2. "Is there a way out of seeking?"—A way out for whom?
3. Every path is the best or the worst path. The What-is is the path.
4. There is no better or best path. Enlightenment is without comparison.
5. Being on a path or not, enlightenment can happen to anybody, at any time, anywhere.
6. *Advaita*: the lazy seeker's path to enlightenment.

## 47. Phenomenality

**(*See* Manifestation)**

1. Prior to phenomenality there is no creation, no dissolution, no path, no goal, no free will, no predestination.
2. Phenomenality is the functioning of Totality, Consciousness or God.
3. Phenomenality is God-in-action.
4. God is in charge of phenomenality.
5. Everything is possible in phenomenality.
6. *Nirvana* in action is *samsara*.
7. What the scriptures describe is the mechanics of

*samsara* or phenomenality.

8. What is written in the *Bhagavad Gita* concerns phenomenality, the What-is.

9. Phenomenality exists in the same way that a shadow exists. The shadow is not real because its existence depends on the substance called light. However, the shadow is there, and to that extent it is real.

   Phenomenality is not real because its existence depends on the essence called Consciousness. However, phenomenality is there, and to that extent it is real.

## 48. Practice, *Sadhana* and Effort

**(*See* Action; Ego and Doership; Enlightenment; Free Will vs God's Will; "Me"; Meditation; Path)**

1. Question: Is it necessary for a seeker to practice? Answer: Do you need to practice golf?

2. In tennis and in meditation, the coach and the guru respectively will teach you how and what to practice. But such coaching is meant for beginners.

3. OK, so you must do *sadhana*! But understand that there is no "you."

4. There is no "one" who can be encouraged or discouraged to do *sadhana*.

5. You say, "I must control my anger."—Who is to control what anger?

6. The individual thinks, "I am doing *sadhana*;

therefore, I am entitled to enlightenment."—This is a wrong expectation.

7. In true *sadhana*, there is no individual doing *sadhana*.
8. There is no practice. Teaching, listening, understanding, enlightenment—they all just happen.
9. Listening is a *sadhana*. But really there is no "one" who listens.
10. Teaching and listening are one event that just happens. Understanding and enlightenment are events that just happen. There is no achievement by any individual. The guru and the disciple are not individuals.
11. No individual seeker can achieve enlightenment. And enlightenment can happen no matter how much, or how little, or what kind of *sadhana* has been done.
12. *Sadhana* and enlightenment are destined; *sadhana* does not produce enlightenment.
13. If enlightenment is destined, it will happen with or without practicing.
14. *Sadhana* and enlightenment are happenings just as storms and earthquakes are.
15. A *puja* or any other *sadhana* is done by the same One who fulfills or does not fulfill what you are asking for.
16. Pilgrimages, *pujas*, *japas* and meditation are for the beginner.
17. *Bhajans* are spiritual rock-concerts.

18. *Satsang* is entertainment for the heart.
19. The most powerful spiritual methods are surrender and Self-inquiry; but Self-inquiry is not a practice.
20. Chicken or beef? No need to worry! Enlightenment has no causes.
21. If the guru teaches free will and effort, he gives the disciple something to hang on to.
22. A list of do's and don'ts and the promise that you will get enlightened by following them is a con-trick.
23. Every morning, the "should's," "could's," "would's" arise.
24. "Should's" or "should not's": for the human mind nothing is ever good enough.
25. The seeker can't do anything right or wrong.
26. Question: Is practicing an enhancement or an obstacle to enlightenment? Answer: It can be both, but whatever it is, it is destined.
27. You cannot practice the teaching because there is no "you."
28. The good news is that enlightenment can happen even if one is practicing a wrong practice towards a wrong goal. Why? Because it is so destined.
29. The bottom line and the final understanding regarding practice are: "I can't do anything about enlightenment."
30. Do whatever you think you are doing until you stop thinking it is "you" who is doing it.
31. The seeker hopes to gain something from the guru that he can use to achieve enlightenment.

32. Giving to and pleasing the guru can enhance the disciple's advancement on his spiritual path.
33. The disciple's urge to give money to the guru does not depend on the need of the guru to receive.
34. No practice is needed for enlightenment to happen. Break all the rules! Don't practice!—if you can.

## 49. Prayer

1. Because the human being cannot get what it wants, it creates the concept of God and prays to Him, "Give me this, don't give me that."
2. Praying means begging and bargaining with God.
3. You cannot bargain with God by doing a *puja* or a good deed.
4. The bargain is: "If I am good, God will be good to me too."
5. The formula "This for that" doesn't work with God. The only true prayer is "Thy Will be done."

## 50. Process and Progress

(*See* Enlightenment; Meditation; Path; Practice)

1. The process of understanding can only advance forward.
2. The process of disidentification occurs in phenomenality.

3. Spiritual progress is a process occurring in Consciousness.
4. The process of disidentification is a process in time, perhaps through billions of body-mind organisms' lives. However, enlightenment always happens suddenly and not in time.
5. The disidentification process continues through many lives—but these are not lives of the same entity!
6. There is good and bad news for the seeker regarding the process of disidentification: it can occur in a hundred steps, or in one single quantum jump.
7. Spiritual progress runs on automatic pilot.
8. Nothing can be gained or lost.
9. In the process of disidentification, everything drops off, including enlightenment.
10. "What is a glimpse?"—It is a glimpse of What-is.
11. If you know the stage you are at in the process of disidentification, then you have not really understood the teaching.
12. The yardsticks of spiritual progress are generosity and forgiveness.
13. Spiritual progress results in a change of attitude. And the change of attitude is a change in the programming—it is a reprogramming.
14. Judgment/non-judgment is the yardstick for spiritual understanding.
15. Witnessing and judgment alternate during the search.

16. The advanced seeker's attitude towards events in life is: "This too will pass."

## 51. Programming

(*See* **Body-Mind Organism; Destiny; Ego and Doership; "Me"**)

1. Electricity functions through a mixer. It is an electrical gadget which is programmed to perform specific tasks. Similarly, each body-mind organism is programmed to function in specific ways and to perform certain reactions.

2. Electricity can function and produce light only when the instrument "lamp" is in place. Similarly, Consciousness can function and produce actions only when its instrument, the sentient being, is in place.

3. The programming of a body-mind organism produces a certain reaction to a specific input—a thought or an event.

4. One's destiny and programming are both willed by God and stamped at conception.

5. The body-mind organism is programmed for enlightenment to happen or not. The program is destined.

6. Your luck is programmed.

## 52. Reality

### (See *Maya*; Truth)

1. Adi Shankara distinguishes between the real and the unreal thus: "That which does not exist at all times is unreal."
2. What you really are is prior to consciousness.
3. The Real must be able to exist by itself.
4. What you are cannot be changed.
5. Janine cannot know Reality because she is Reality.
6. Whatever exists now, existed in phenomenality a thousand years ago, and will exist a thousand years from now.
7. "Now" doesn't change.
8. Nothing has ever happened really. There is no creation. There is no dissolution. There is no path. There is no goal. There is no destiny. There is no free will. There truly is no seeker.
9. What exists in deep sleep is Reality.
10. Only what exists in deep sleep is real. The ordinary person has the wrong understanding that the world keeps existing for others while he is asleep; but his personal experience during sleep is that nothing exists. However, it is the impersonal awareness during sleep that enables him to know how he slept. Because, during sleep, there is no personal awareness of sleeping, sleep cannot be experienced. It could only be experienced by a "me."
11. Whatever does not exist in deep sleep is an illusion.

12. In deep sleep there is no illusion.

## 53. Right and Wrong—Good and Bad

(*See* Life)

1. The same event can be both good and bad. Christmas is beautiful for the human being. But what about the turkey?
2. When the smallpox germ is eliminated, it is good for the human being and bad for the germ.
3. While in the working mind, there is no good and no bad. Therefore, work is worship.
4. Doing the right or wrong thing makes no difference. Both are destined.
5. Advice given by the *jnani* may turn out to be good or bad, and that is destined.
6. Good intentions may lead you to hell, and bad intentions may be the road to heaven. Why? Because it is so destined.
7. You say, "The world is bad." God made the world. Let Him take care of it!

## 54. Sage/Jnani

(*See* Guru; Enlightenment)

1. The sage is part of phenomenality.
2. "What makes a saint a saint?"—He has no sense of

personal doership.

3. What all sages have in common is the annihilation of personal doership.

4. The sage's "mode" in phenomenality is "living without the sense of personal doership."

5. The sage behaves like a dry leaf in the wind.

6. The good man is not aware that he is good.

7. The four stages of the sage are the working mind, witnessing, non-witnessing and *samadhi*.

8. In the sage, the "I-Am"-in-action is constantly occurring as witnessing.

9. Anger may arise in a sage; but in his case there is no reaction to the arising of anger.

10. The sage's anger or worry is natural—*prakriti* (nature; impersonal energy). The sage is not a vegetable.

11. Nisargadatta Maharaj: the quick-tempered *jnani*.

12. The sage has no control over the arising of a thought. After a thought has arisen, there is no involvement in further thinking in his case.

13. The *jnani* accepts love and hate as the basis of life.

14. For the sage there is no "him," and therefore, no love nor hate.

15. The sage's life also has ups and downs, but without the sense of personal doership.

16. After enlightenment the sage stays identified with the body-mind organism and the name. However, in his case, the identification as an individual doer has ceased.

17. The *jnani* may take money because he doesn't expect or refuse anything.
18. Question: If the sage has absolute and total awareness, can he still trip and break his leg? Answer: Even a mindful sage can break his leg.
19. The sage has no additional or exclusive source of knowledge.
20. The seeker asks the guru, "Are you the Whole? Are you in connection with the Whole?"—The guru answers, "All there is, is Consciousness."
21. In the sage's understanding, talking and listening are one event.
22. The sage's enlightenment brings about the peace of acceptance. It is not a permanent blissful state.
23. The thought of death can arise in a sage. But the personal doer is already dead.
24. At death, the impersonal Consciousness of the sage becomes Consciousness-at-rest.
25. The realized one knows that he was never born. How then can he die?

## The Sage and The Non-sage

1. The sage sees the world exactly like the seeker. However, he knows that whatever is functioning in manifestation is God's Will.
2. The sage and the non-sage are functioning in exactly the same way. However, the sage has no sense of personal doership.

3. "I am angry" (the seeker) versus "There is anger" (the sage).
4. The sage and the ordinary person are both slaves of the functioning of Totality:
5. A dream, a vision, a thought, a feeling—all occurrences are beyond control for the sage and the non-sage alike.
6. In deep sleep, pure Subjectivity prevails for the sage and the ordinary person alike.
7. In deep sleep, the sage, like the non-sage, cannot be aware of his body or of manifestation.
8. The non-separation of the child from Totality is ignorance. The non-separation of the *jnani* is knowledge.
9. The child is enlightenment plus ignorance. The sage is enlightenment plus knowledge.

## 55. *Samadhi*

1. *Samadhi* is a kind of wakeful sleep. The body is awake and consciousness is asleep.
2. *Samadhi* is physical wakefulness plus "deep sleep."

## 56. *Sat-Chit-Ananda*

1. *Sat-Chit-Ananda* (Truth-Consciousness-Bliss) is not an object to be had by an individual.
2. *Sat-Chit-Ananda* is a concept, not something to be gotten.

## 57. Science

1. The scientist is very well paid for wondering.
2. In the West, science replaced God. It became a religion—as God intended.
3. Question: What is the place of science within spirituality? Answer: Science is part of life and phenomenality. It tries to explain the functioning or the mechanics of life.

## 58. Seeker

### (*See* Seeking)

1. Physical and mental health is a must for the successful seeker.
2. The seeker says, "I have a stupid question." The guru answers, "All questions are stupid."
3. Ramana Maharshi's comment describes every seeker's situation: "Your head is already in the tiger's mouth."
4. There is no seeker—seeking just happens.
5. It is not true that the seeker is seeking. Consciousness has created the seeker, made him seek, and is seeking through him.
6. The seeker is already what he seeks. God is seeking Himself as the seeker.
7. The seeker is like the stick that is used to stir the

funeral pyre. It gets annihilated in the process. And stirring means effort.

8. It is stupid for a guru to demand earnestness and courage from the seeker.

9. "I was lucky not to be a seeker." (*Ramesh*)

## 59. Seeking

### (*See* Seeker)

1. If, how, and when seeking begins, continues and ends is destined.

2. Earnestness in seeking cannot be acquired. You either have it or you don't.

3. God seeks enlightenment through a body-mind organism.

4. Seeking is seeking the source from which manifestation and the seeker arose.

5. Seeking is seeking what is prior to manifestation.

6. Consciousness or God created a body-mind organism with such programming that spiritual seeking is taking place through it.

7. There is no individual seeker—seeking is part of the functioning of Totality.

8. Seeking is an ongoing, independent, impersonal event right from the mother's breast to enlightenment.

9. Seeking is part of the impersonal functioning of Totality, but there is no seeker!

10. In searching, the Subject is seeking the Subject.
11. Seeking takes place because the Sought wants it to.
12. Seeking is not a matter of volition.
13. The same power that seeks Truth also seeks money.
14. God seeks money through a body-mind organism.
15. Seeking begins with an individual and ends with not wanting enlightenment anymore.
16. Unless the seeker gets annihilated, the seeking cannot stop. Wanting never stops unless the seeking stops.
17. For Grace to happen, seeking has to stop. But the seeking stops only by Grace. It is a double-bind.
18. The process of seeking starts with the individual and continues until there is the total understanding that the individual just doesn't exist.
19. The search ends in the failure of the "me."
20. Seeking means seeking freedom from the "me."
21. "I want the seeking to stop."—Fine! But can you stop seeking before enlightenment occurs?
22. "Seeking is misery. That's why I'm giving it up."— You can't give it up! The seeking has got hold of you.
23. Seeking means suffering.
24. Seeking happiness is unhappiness.
25. "Must I feel passionately about seeking?"—Why should you?
26. Seeking takes a different form in every seeker; its intensity and strength differ from seeker to seeker.
27. Seeking means not accepting What-is and how and what you are.

28. Seeking means you want to change What-is and become what you are not.
29. The seeker's ego says the search for enlightenment is far superior to the search for money.
30. You say you are looking for Truth, not for meaning. Who is to find Truth?
31. If you seek something that is not an object, you still seek an illusion. The act of seeking is part of that illusion.
32. The nature of seeking is, "I can't hasten it, and I can't stop it."
33. You may understand that there is no difference between being enlightened or not. However, can you stop seeking?
34. I tell you, enlightenment is truly boring. Now stop seeking it if you can!
35. When the seeking stops, the What-is remains; in other words, "All there is, is Consciousness."

## 60. Self-Inquiry

1. At some point the mind turns inward and asks, "Who or what am I?"
2. Who are you? Who is the questioner? Who wants to know? Where and what is the mind?—Find out!

## 61. Silence

1. Listening without grabbing what is heard, is silence.

2. When questioning stops, silence happens; when silence happens, seeking stops.
3. Words are mental concepts; silence is the ultimate teaching.
4. The ultimate and the finest teaching is silence.

## 62. Spirituality

1. In true spirituality, there is no "how to."
2. True spirituality has no prescriptions, only descriptions.
3. Surrender is a dirty word in life, but a magnificent word in spirituality.
4. Spiritual awakening means that the nightmares and pleasures of the living dream called life don't really matter anymore.

## 63. Suffering

### (*See* Happiness)

1. "Why does God create misery?"—Why not! Life is a combination of opposites.
2. The "me" is suffering misery and bliss.
3. You are doomed to misery by destiny—and you are only 25!
4. The phenomenal manifestation is dream-like and not real. This realization stops suffering.

5. The degree of suffering depends on the degree of involvement.
6. Question: Is there a way out of suffering? Answer: A way out of what? All there is, is Consciousness. You can't do a damn thing to get out. There is no "in" and no "out." There is no "you"!
7. There is a way out of suffering only if it is so destined.
8. "I am searching for the end of suffering."—Your search is in vain.
9. The misery and the bliss of the seeker have no meaning; they just happen.
10. Because you are suffering to the point of death, you may say, "Now I am eligible for enlightenment."—Ha, ha, ha!
11. Consciousness *is* the bliss or misery. Consciousness cannot enjoy bliss or suffer misery.
12. After enlightenment, physical and mental suffering may continue; however, there is no one to suffer them.
13. The sage doesn't enjoy bliss or suffer misery because "he" is not involved.

## 64. The Teaching

### (*See* Understanding)

1. The teaching in a nutshell: "Thy Will be done."
2. The gist of the teaching is "All there is, is Consciousness."

3. The teaching is only a description of What-is. It is not a prescription.

4. The teaching has no prescriptions regarding *sadhana*, methods or practices. It merely describes What-is. When the What-is is accepted, nothing further needs to be done.

5. You cannot use the teaching to solve your problems.

6. The teaching is not a tool for becoming happy.

7. You cannot make use of what you have heard of the teaching.

8. The teaching cannot be used as an instrument for change.

9. To suggest how you should live your life is a wrong teaching.

10. The teaching is no good if life does not become simpler because of it.

11. The effect of the teaching is that life becomes not easier, but simpler.

12. "Does the teaching make life easier for the seeker?"—Simpler, yes; easier, yes and no.

13. The result of listening to the teaching is: no feeling of pride, guilt, or enmity.

14. If life doesn't become simpler through the teaching, the latter is useless.

15. This teaching is a self-destructive process. In the process of seeking, the "me" gets annihilated.

16. This teaching is a self-destructive process. The ego gets annihilated by the understanding.

17. The teaching brings about the end of all experiences.

18. Any teaching that tells you how to live your life is addressed to the individual.
19. The guru's lie may be what the seeker needs. His lie can be the teaching.
20. "My way of practice is the only way to enlightenment" is a wrong teaching.
21. "How do you know that what you say is true?"— I don't!
22. Question: Are your talks intended to teach the Truth? Answer: No, they are merely an event.
23. The talks here are an impersonal event.
24. After you have heard the teaching, the sage suggests, "Keep doing what you like," because what you will do is God's Will anyway. However, what you like may not happen.
25. It is good to forget the teaching because it can't go anywhere except deeper.
26. The guru's final teaching weapon in response to any question is the counter-question, "Who wants to know?"
27. If you are programmed to kill, you won't feel the need for any teaching.

## 65. Thinking Mind vs Working Mind

### (*See* Mind; Witnessing)

1. Seeking is done by the thinking mind.
2. The average person is continuously involved in the thinking mind.

3. Absent-mindedness is an aspect of the thinking mind; mindfulness is an aspect of the working mind.
4. Words are the vocalizations of thought, and their interpretation is mental involvement by the thinking mind.
5. Thinking is conceptualizing. Day-dreaming is thinking in pictures related to the feeling of "me."
6. The cutting off of involvement in thinking occurs when the thought "There was involvement" arises from outside. It is an impersonal event.
7. The realization that one has been involved in the thinking mind comes all of a sudden.
8. Consciousness-in-action is understanding. Understanding-in-action is the sudden realization "There was involvement."
9. Did I say it is easy not to be involved? It is not!
10. In the absence of horizontal involvement with the thinking mind, either the working mind, witnessing or the non-witnessing state occur.
11. Thinking mind: one's work is interrupted by doubts, fears, desires, worries and thoughts regarding good or bad future consequences. Working mind: one has total concentration on the job at hand, without concern for the outcome or the future consequences.
12. As long as the working mind is in motion, the thinking mind is on holiday.
13. While the working mind is in operation, the thinking mind is out of work.
14. When there is no thinking mind, work is worship.

15. Lucky you, if you have a job that you like. Why? Because while working, you are in the working mind.
16. Question: Do I watch TV with the working mind? Answer: The concept doesn't apply to this activity. The concept of the working mind is used for the actual activity of working.
17. The working mind is something like going to the toilet.
18. "Be still and free from thought" means "Be free from the thinking mind."

## 66. Thought and Memory

### (See Body-Mind Organism)

1. Memory and mind are different faculties of the body-mind organism.
2. Every experience is impersonal; memory is personal.
3. Memory exists in deep sleep.
4. All thoughts concern phenomenality.
5. You can't create a thought.
6. The brain receives a thought, it doesn't create it.
7. The brain is inert matter. It cannot create a thought.
8. The brain cannot create a thought. It can only react to an outside impulse.
9. Thought is not part of the body-mind organism. The state of coma proves this fact. In a coma, the brain doesn't work.
10. Thought is connected with Consciousness and not with the body.

11. A thought can appear from memory. The brain reacts to it and the body-mind organism produces a reaction. Is it your thought and your action, or is it God's? It is God's.

12. It makes no difference if a thought comes from memory and is repeated, or if it is a new thought. A thought comes from "outside," from Consciousness.

13. Memory and thoughts are outside impulses—they are not produced by the brain.

14. Question: Do thoughts come from inside or from outside? Answer: Inside/outside exists only from the point of view of the individual. The Creator is the whole creation. From His point of view there is no inside or outside.

15. Most meditators entertain the wrong notion that their practice will slow down the thought flow and finally make it stop altogether when the goal of enlightenment is reached. Even after the "me" with its sense of personal doership is annihilated forever in the occurrence of enlightenment, the arising of thoughts can never be prevented.

## 67. Truth

### (See *Maya*; Reality)

1. "Is the purpose of life to find Truth?"—The purpose of life for whom? Who is to find Truth?

2. "Aren't we already Truth?"—Truth is What-is at this moment.

3. In a review of one's life, one will keep saying, "It so happened that..." That is the truth.

## 68. Understanding

### (*See* The Teaching)

1. Understanding is God.
2. The ultimate understanding is accepting What-is.
3. Understanding-in-action is impersonal witnessing.
4. The final understanding is the acceptance of What-is as the functioning of Totality or God. However, that acceptance is not in your hands.
5. In the final understanding, there is no surrenderer, no accepter, no seeker and no finder.
6. You know you have understood the teaching when questions answer themselves.
7. You know you have understood the teaching when questions don't matter anymore and they dissolve.
8. The stopping of all questioning is the most powerful understanding.
9. Understanding means there is no need for understanding.
10. The understanding "Thy Will be done" is the end of all questions.
11. The understanding brings about freedom from pride, guilt and enmity.
12. For most seekers, the understanding comes and goes.

13. The understanding cannot be used as a tool to better one's life.

14. You cannot use the understanding to change your conduct and behavior.

15. The understanding deepens when this attitude evolves: "I don't care what happens," or, "It doesn't matter what happens."

16. "It so happened that...," "It doesn't really matter," and "So be it!" are expressions of a deepening understanding

17. It doesn't matter if success or failure occurs; the understanding "Thy Will be done" brings about freedom from responsibility for both.

18. The seeker's penultimate understanding, prior to enlightenment is: a) "I did all I could;" b) "I am not enlightened yet;" and c) "Now I don't care about enlightenment anymore, and I just do whatever I feel like doing."

19. The penultimate state before enlightenment is the acceptance that enlightenment may not happen.

20. The penultimate understanding before enlightenment is: "All right, God, if You don't want to bring about enlightenment in this body-mind organism, don't! I don't care if enlightenment happens or not. Everything happens according to Your Will."

21. The understanding "Thy Will be done" will not let you sit idle.

## 69. Waking State (Living Dream)

### (*See* Deep Sleep State; Dream State)

1. You wake up from your personal dream (the dream state) into your living dream (the waking state).
2. Waking up from sleep and the appearance of manifestation are simultaneous and synonymous.
3. On waking up, awareness and the body-mind organism appear together.
4. Without space no object can be projected. Without time no projected object can be perceived. Space/time is the mechanism through which the personal dream and the living dream happen.
5. The dreamer of the living dream is Consciousness; the script writer of the dream is Consciousness; all characters are played by Consciousness; all objects are Consciousness; what is aware of the dream is Consciousness.
6. The individual who observes the living dream is part of the movie.
7. The living dream appears and continues for the dreamer, i.e. for anyone who is awake.
8. All personal dreams differ; the living dream is shared with others; but in both there is no free will.
9. The living dream has no meaning.
10. The only way to switch off the living dream is through death.
11. The living dream can only end with death.

12. Waking up spiritually means realizing that life is a living dream.
13. Life is a living dream in phenomenality. In the original state, nothing has ever happened.

## 70. What-Is

### (*See* Acceptance; All there is, is Consciousness; Being; Destiny; Free Will vs God's Will)

1. The What-is is not concerned with any particular person.
2. What-is at the present moment is God's Will.
3. There is nothing except What-is.
4. "God is love" describes only half the truth. What-is —Consciousness—is both love and hate.
5. You say, "There's a mess." It is part of What-is. Who created it? God.
6. "Now" doesn't change.

## 71. Witnessing

### (*See* Judgement; Thinking Mind vs Working Mind)

1. You want to observe your thoughts! Who is to observe the thoughts? The mind observes its own working.
2. "You" cannot witness. "You" can only observe.

3. Witnessing happens whenever the thinking mind is absent.
4. Witnessing is "sleeping while being awake," because the "me," the personal doer, is asleep.
5. When insulted, the ordinary person gets involved but the sage keeps witnessing.
6. Did I say it is easy not to be involved? It is not!
7. Choice means not witnessing.
8. Witnessing is accepting What-is as it is.
9. Witnessing is done by the same Power that created the body-mind organism.
10. Consciousness witnesses whatever is happening through a body-mind organism.
11. Witnessing is an impersonal happening. God or Consciousness is witnessing what It is creating or what It has created.
12. In witnessing, the subject and the object are one.
13. When the understanding "Thy Will be done" occurs, a witnessing attitude will become your habit and life-style.

## Non-Witnessing

1. In the non-witnessing state, there is nothing to witness.
2. Non-witnessing is the human being's natural state.

# Part 2

# Friendly Sword

Ramesh S. Balsekar Answers 24 Key
Questions (Recorded at the Kovalam
Beach Seminar, 1994)

Session at the Kovalam Beach Seminar 1995

Ramesh had been talking to a lady visitor from Sweden for most of the morning session. When she was about to leave, she thanked him and said:

Lady: *What you did was amazing! Each of your answers to my questions was like a sword blow that not only annihilated the question but was cutting pieces of my mind away with it.*

Ramesh: Aha! That's what the teaching is supposed to do and does. That's right.

Lady: *You seemed to know exactly where to cut and how much at the time.*

Ramesh: The teaching is doing the cutting. I am only holding the sword.

Lady: *It felt like a clinical operation was occurring in which I was being operated upon. Now I feel totally unburdened, cleaned, new and fresh, and completely freed of the mind. It is miraculous. Thank you.*

# Introductory Note

This short but wide-ranging chapter presents an overview of the main tenets of Ramesh's teaching. It features Ramesh's answers to 24 key questions put to him by the Editor at a seminar given in the idyllic surroundings of Kovalam Beach, Kerala, India. The extracts cited provide a vivid illustration of Ramesh's teaching style which is both uncompromising and at the same time endearingly easy-going.

Some of the slogan-like tenets presented in *Gentle Hammer* are taken up again here, and elaborated on in the conversations between the seeker Madhukar and his guru Ramesh. In contrast with the turbulent effect generated by the repeated hammer blows of the Gentle Hammer, the tone of this chapter is calmer and more human, and as they unfold, the exchanges become more personal, almost intimate.

In the dialogues, Ramesh may be seen as a mild-mannered samurai warrior, wielding his Sword of Understanding with graceful strokes which dispatch the seeker's questions one by one. The samurai and his "victim" perform their designated roles smoothly, as Truth cuts through the questioner's illusions. Their "duel" will only end when a blow of the sword, as destined, cuts the seeker's question, and the very impulse driving his heart-felt inquiries, right back to the Source from which they, and all the answers and answering too, arose. Until this happens, more questions arise as soon as one is answered. Just as from the severed head of a hydra new heads sprout, so new questions keep arising in a seeker's mind. No problem! Ramesh, the tireless samurai, keeps striking his sword at them with masterly skill. He will probably go on doing so until he breathes his last, or until (as happens in some cases) the seeker-entity and, with it, all questioning and all sense of personal volition and doership, are annihilated once and for all and the erstwhile seeker remains fully rooted in his own true nature, the Source.

# 1. By Inquiring "Who am I?" the Seeker is Really Asking, "Who is the 'Me'?"

Q (Madhukar): *The nature of my practice of Self-inquiry seems to have changed. When I first began inquiring, it was the individual, personal "I," the ego, that was asking the question "Who am I?" Although there was no verbal answer, there instead was a nothingness as an answer. Then, after some time, the inquiry was repeated by the ego-"I," producing the same "answer." But the ego-"I" never got annihilated for good. It always arose again.*

*Lately, during the Self-inquiry, "Who am I?", the ego-"I" is kind of fading away and dissolving into a nothing which at the same time seems a sort of impersonal non-object which could be called the "I" of "all or everything." I can't really describe with words what exactly happens. My question is, is what I have described as the remaining "answer," is that the "I-I"?*

A (Ramesh): You speak of the inquiry "Who am I?" Really, the question should actually be, "Who is this 'me'?" You see?

Q: *Can you make it clearer?*

A: The question "Who am I?" points in the same direction as the question "Who is wanting to know what or who it is?" does.

Q: *The question itself contains the ego, the personal "I," because it is asked by the ego. After a couple of months of practicing Self-inquiry, the "I" which asks began to dissolve into an impersonal "all-I" during the actual inquiry.*

A: That may happen momentarily. But it is always the "me" who is trying to become the impersonal "I." Therefore, there is still the "me" trying to become the "I." What will be found out through Self-inquiry? That the "me" can never be an "I." The "I" is all there is. The "me" kind of eclipses the "I-I." Ramana Maharshi's point was, "Find out who is this "me" who wants to know?" And you will come to know that the "me" never existed. He made it perfectly clear that Self-inquiry is not a *sadhana*. It is not a *sadhana* in the sense that you take a *mala*, and you keep repeating "Who am I? Who am I? Who am I?" like a *mantra*. That is not the intention of Self-inquiry at all. The intention is to find out, who this "me" is that is seeking. Who is this "me" that wants something? And when you concentrate on the question, "Who is this 'me'?" or "What is this 'me'?", then the question itself drops. There is no answer to the question. And when the mind finds out that there is no answer, it comes to the conclusion that there is no "me." Because the question dissolves, along with the "me" which questions. So, Ramana Maharshi calls Self-inquiry the most direct path. It simply leads to the conclusion that there is no "me."

114

Q: *In that understanding all questions drop, right?*

A: That is the point: the question drops. And when the question drops, the questioner is no longer there. The question will remain so long as the questioner is there. So when the question drops the questioner is also gone. But Ramana Maharshi makes it perfectly clear that questioning will happen again and again and again. But the more the question remains unanswered, the less it will arise. Over time, and with practice, the frequency with which the question is asked becomes gradually less and less.

## 2. "I Am in Ecstasy" is Dualism—"There is Ecstasy" is Duality

Q: *I have a question regarding bliss. Let us say ecstasy or bliss arises in this body mind organism and...*

A: Yes.

Q: *Do I perceive it correctly that at the time of its arising, there is also an awareness of its arising. Are awareness and bliss present at the same time?*

A: Yes.

Q: *The arising of bliss in the body-mind system and the*

*awareness of this bliss seem to happen at the same time.*

A: Yes.

Q: *Because there is awareness of something else, i.e. bliss, is that why you call that occurrence a happening in duality?*

A: Yes, that is duality not dualism. It is duality when there is awareness of an ecstasy. The awareness of that ecstasy is duality. "I am in ecstasy" is dualism.

Q: *If the "I" is not there—if there is awareness and ecstasy at the same time without a "me"—is that still duality?*

A: Yes, that is duality, because it is still happening in phenomenality. What I call dualism is when I say, "'I' am in ecstasy. It is a wonderful feeling. I want it again." "I am in ecstasy," is dualism. But to say, "There is an awareness of ecstasy—without the 'me,'" is duality.

Q: *Duality is what happens without the "me." Therefore, duality happens all the time. It is only interrupted by the "me-thought" and other thoughts.*

A: That is correct.

Q: *Is this what you experience at this very moment?*

A: Yes, sure! Of course!

So long as there is phenomenal manifestation and its functioning, it always has to be in duality.

Q: *My question always was: who is perceiving the awareness and the ecstasy? The ecstasy happens, the awareness of it is present, and I keep questioning myself: who is the one who is perceiving it? Who is the perceiver?*

A: So long as there is an individual perceiver, it is dualism. When the question "Who is perceiving?" doesn't arise at all, then that is duality. So long as the question "Who is perceiving?" is there, the ego is there, the "who" is there, the dualism is there.

Q: *So there seems to be a very fine line, or a sudden moment in which the "me" attaches itself to pure Awareness and covers it with its egoism by saying "I am blissful." And so the impersonal "There is awareness of bliss" becomes personal.*

A: That is absolutely correct. Well, Madhukar, you can call it a very fine line or a mile-thick line. *(laughter)*

## 3. Enlightenment: A feeling of Oneness in Duality

Q: *In my spiritual search so far, I have tended to put the guru somewhere high, high up there. Either that, or the guru placed himself high up there. However, I notice a difference here. Now, being with you and in your presence, all is very natural and ordinary. I feel there is a simple suchness about you sitting there and me sitting here. And that's about all. Nothing spectacular or extraordinary about it. This "me" putting the guru organism over there up into the sky, has relaxed. My desire to be enlightened like you has weakened. I feel I am just here with you in suchness.*

A: Are you making a statement or...? *(laughter)*

Q: *Well, yes. I just realized that I was making one.* (laughter)

A: As I said, the process of disidentification goes on continuously. There is a most beautiful chapter on the guru-disciple relationship in the book *Amritanubhava* written by Gyaneshwar. *Amrit* means immortality, *anubhava* means experience. So the literal translation is "experience of immortality." I am afraid my book with the same title—*Experience of Immortality*[1]—is out of print. In the chapter called "The Guru-Disciple Relationship" Gyaneshwar writes so lovingly. He says, "I understand my guru knew that he and I were one. Now I also understand that I and my guru are one. Nonetheless, so long as this body-mind organism exists in phenomenality, this organism will continue to respect the other organism as his guru. Yet I understand fully that there is no difference between the two of us. I understand fully that both organisms are the objective

---

[1] Published by Chetana, Bombay, 1984

representation of that Supreme Oneness."

So, the love for the guru never really disappears. "Love for the guru" really means "love for Consciousness." So long as the body exists, so long as the feeling of being an organism is there, there will always be a sense of oneness. And yet the duality will always be there as long there is phenomenality.

When enlightenment happens, the individual sense of doership will drop off. On the other hand, so long as the body exists in phenomenality, the feeling of love or ecstasy, the love for the guru, keeps on arising. The love for the guru truly never disappears. However, it is not the love that one entity has for another entity. It is the love which is the basic essence of Consciousness as such. That is what is realized.

## 4. The Ultimate Understanding: The Absence of Conceptualizing

Q: *The "I am" can be experienced directly as my own being. But I don't know what you mean with the "I-I." I don't know it because it is not my own experience. I hear you speak about the "I-I." I heard Ramana Maharshi speak about it. In my case the "I-I" has no direct existential actuality because I haven't experienced it yet. Can it be experienced at all, and how? Do you experience it?*

A: There is nothing actual about the "I-I," Madhukar.

That is the whole point. The moment we open our mouths, or the moment we accept a thought and the thinking begins, it is nothing but conceptualizing. It is nothing but creating images in the mind.

Q: *This "I-I," is it also a concept?*

A: Very much so!

Q: *It cannot be seen. It cannot be experienced. Or can it?*

A: Of course not! Speaking about the "I-I," "I am," and "I am Albert," is just a systematical concept.

Q: *It is made up by the mind. Who is making it up? Who is making up the concept, and why? I know some teachers make it up. In the present case it is you who is doing it.*

A: Yes.

Q: *How can one disappear into the "not anything," as an actuality beyond all talking? Do you know what I mean to say?*

A: That happens when the teaching is intuitively understood. In fact, when the intuitive understanding transcends the intellectual understanding, then conceptualization ceases. But until conceptualization ceases, concepts are necessary. Ramana Maharshi makes is quite clear that concepts are necessary. The teacher uses a concept in order to make the pupil understand something. Ramana uses a very nice metaphor. He says a concept is like a thorn that is used to remove another thorn embedded in your foot. But once the thorn is used to remove the embedded thorn, then both thorns are thrown away. When all concepts cease, then there is no need for any concepts. Then conceptualization is transcended.

Therefore, according to Ramana, the ultimate understanding is total silence—which means the absence of conceptualizing.

This morning you were talking about bliss: *Sat-Chit-Ananda*. It is a mere concept which is used to make the disciple understand that whatever he is seeking is still a concept. *Sat-Chit-Ananda* denotes the bliss that transcends material enjoyment and ecstasy. But speaking about it is still concept. And unless the concept is given up, or rather, gets given up, the total understanding cannot happen. The total understanding means the absence of all problems, the absence of all conceptualizing, the absence of anything that seems to matter. The ultimate understanding is that there is no "one" to be concerned about anything.

## 5. The Past, Present and Future are not a Passing Show: They Always Exist

Q: *I hear you say that whatever was, exists here/now;*

*whatever is at this moment, exists here/now; and whatever will be, exists already here/now.*

A: That is correct.

Q: *Do you mean to say that everything exists now but will happen at another time?*

A: That is correct.

Q: *What happens at this moment doesn't appear only once here/now and then fade away, disappearing forever. Is that what you mean to say?*

A: That is correct.

Q: *What you indicate is that although the present happening passes away, it keeps existing somehow, somewhere. Is that why we can have past-life experiences or visions of the past in the here and now?*

A: Quite right, that is correct.

Q: *Even though they actually happened hundreds of years ago?*

A: That's right. And the whole future of the universe also exists already at this present moment. It is already there. That is why some people are able to see into the future. Their ability proves that the future must already be there, doesn't it?

Q: *You are speaking of people like Nostradamus?*

A: Yes. The future exists already. To be able to see something in the future, it has to be there. Otherwise, these people couldn't see it.

## 6. You Cannot Know That Which You Are

Q: *How can the "I-I" be known?*

A: It cannot be known. Why? You can only know something that is different from you, right? If Consciousness or "I-I" is all there is, who could know Consciousness? Consciousness is all there is. Therefore no one can know that state. We can only *be* that state.

Q: *Can anybody know it? How do you know it? If you can't know it and you don't know it, how can you speak about it and tell us as if you know it?*

A: Nobody can know it. That is why the moment you utter a word, it is not the Truth. You *are* the Truth. Therefore, the sage is not concerned with imparting knowledge. However, the guru has to talk and teach because the disciple comes to him and asks questions.

But all talking and all listening are part of phenomenality. You cannot *know* that which you *are*
yourself—I don't mean the body-mind organism called
Madhukar, but that which *is*.

If Consciousness is all there is, then "who" or
"what" can know Consciousness? If Truth—the "I-I"—
is all there is, how could anyone know that which is
the only thing?

Q: *To know something...*

A: Wait a minute! For me to know something else, the
"me," or the "I," and what I know have to be two, don't
they? Otherwise there is no question of knowing.

Bruce: *So you mean to say that the active understanding is
not an active knowledge.*

A: No, indeed not.

Q: *Are actual seeing, and hearing—pure Seeing, pure Hearing
without interpretation—the closest there is to "I-I"?*

A: No, pure Seeing etc. is closest to "I-Am"—the
functioning of "I-I." "I-I" functions as the "I-Am." And
when the functioning stops, when the Consciousness
that has arisen on the "I-I" finishes, it goes back to the
Potential. The potential Energy that has activated itself
at the moment of the Big Bang goes back into the

Potential once the Big Bang—the activation of the energy—has run its full course and has spent itself. However, the "I-Am" appears again from the "I-I" as long as a body exists.

Mind you, the activation of potential Energy is a concept. Anything in the activated form, anything in phenomenality, has got to be just a concept. The "I-I" and the "I-Am" are concepts too. All concepts disappear into total silence. And that total silence is the "I-I" in phenomenality. "I am Madhukar" becomes "I-Am" which is the understanding; but even the understanding depends on the phenomenal body. So long as the phenomenal body is there, the "I-Am" is there, which is impersonal Consciousness. And that impersonal Consciousness disappears only when the body dies.

Let me repeat: no one, sage or non-sage, can know the "I-I" because you *are* the "I-I." For someone to know something, there has to be two, isn't it so? If Consciousness is all there is, how could it be known to anything else. There is nothing other than Consciousness.

### 7. Mind Is *Maya's* Instrument—Mind Cannot Transcend *Maya*

Q: *For me so called well-being or bliss seems to be a trap into which I fall again and again, because I keep desiring it again as soon as the good feeling has faded away. It seems that the ego, the "me" is not present in bliss, or less present than it is in misery. In misery the ego is felt very strongly.*

*Bliss just appears. It doesn't take any effort to be in bliss. When I try to hold on to it, it is gone. And there seems to be no way to hold on to it. I wish I could, but no matter how hard I try, it disappears. Bliss is gone almost immediately when the feeling of it has come to an end. And when the feeling of bliss has past, it is gone completely. Soon after, it is even difficult to remember its intensity.*

*Not so with the feeling of misery. After misery has been triggered, it seems to last much longer in time than bliss does. It seems that the ego has to work much longer and harder through the bad patch. I want the feeling of pain to go away as soon as possible. But it doesn't. It seems to take much more effort and time to be in misery, and to go through it, than it takes to be in bliss.*

A: Sure, yes.

Q: *For me, the desire for bliss and well-being seems to be always there. This desire is and was, I guess, the main reason for me to go to a master. I heard that he is eternally blissful. I wanted the same thing. I wanted him to tell me how I could become like him. I wanted him to tell me what I had to do in order to reach the same permanent blissful state that he enjoyed. Being with these masters I could actually experience a lot of bliss.*

*But because this bliss was not permanent, the desire for it became a problem. The more bliss I experienced the more I* wanted it to be permanent. Moments of bliss, even many of them, were not enough. I demanded permanent bliss because I heard that it can be had. No amount of bliss was enough as long as it fell short of permanency. I got stuck with this particular desire.

I hear you say that life becomes simple when there is no "me" in both extremes, bliss and misery. I hear you say that mere witnessing of whatever happens will cut off the involvement with all desired and undesired feelings. I am sure that you are right and that witnessing does the job. I wish I could just witness everything without getting involved. But for me that doesn't work yet. I also know that witnessing cannot be learned or done volitionally.

A: No, it can't. That is the whole point.

Q: OK, so nothing can be done. What to do, then?

A: The whole point, Madhukar, is that you are pursuing bliss. You said it straight away at the very beginning. The mind is pursuing bliss. Whether the mind is pursuing bliss, or the mind and body-mind organism together are pursuing a million dollars, makes no difference. I have always said, "If you had the choice (and you do not have the choice) of going after a million dollars, go after the million dollars." Because when you get the money, there will be a "Madhukar" to enjoy the million dollars. On the other hand, when the real bliss of non-involvement happens,

127

there will be no Madhukar to enjoy the bliss.

So long as there is a "Madhukar" pursuing something called "bliss," the end can never happen. Pursuing bliss is just a notion, an illusion. And this is the only thing to be understood: so long as there is a pursuer, pursuing the object of pursuit, nothing can happen, nothing worthwhile can happen. You speak about suffering. I feel with you. I'm not being insensitive. I understand you exactly, because I've gone through it too. I have gone through the same frustration. I remember you asked me some time ago what the secret of my happy marriage with Sharda is. I told you, "It is destiny." (*laughter*)

One has to accept that what one wants is merely a matter of destiny. And it also is a matter of destiny whether one will get what one wants or not. Wanting it and not getting it, or wanting it and getting it and being happy, or wanting something and not getting it and being frustrated, is destined. What do you think *maya* means other than this? This is *maya,* which has been spoken about so often and so freely without really understanding what it is. The mind cannot get out of *maya* through its own will and efforts. In fact, the mind is the instrument that *maya* uses. *Maya* works through the mind. Therefore, it is impossible for the mind to transcend *maya.* That is the whole understanding.

Q: *That means there is no way out. "I" cannot get out of it. "I" cannot do anything volitionally to get out of* maya.

A: That is the point. No individual can do anything about it. It can only happen.

I know it's not terribly helpful, Madhukar. (laughter) But what I say is a fact. It is a fact that I don't have a million dollars. I have to accept that. I know that I am not six foot four inches tall, and that I am not an Arnold Schwarzenegger. I have to accept the fact. If I don't accept that fact, and instead I pursue the impossible, I will end up in frustration, no matter what I do about it.

## 8. "God, Who are You?"—"I-Am," God Replies

Q: *I was always wondering what God meant exactly when he said, "I am that I am." The saying is from the Bible. Ramana Maharshi also used to talk about it.*

A: Supposedly, it was said to Moses, wasn't it?

Colin: *It is a quote from the Old Testament. God said it to Moses when He spoke to him at the Burning Bush.*

A: Ramana quoted it as perhaps the most accurate statement about what or who God is. God was asked by Moses, "Who are you?" And God's answer was, "I am that I am." The stress is not on the word "that." It is not "I am *that* I am." He means to say, "I am—that I am." "I am." "I am being." That's it. "I am" is where all explanations finish. "'I am'—that's what I am."

"Being—that's what I am. I am the impersonal Consciousness."

Therefore, God is only "I." "I" is not any objective thing. That is what it means: "I am that I am." You see? It is not: "I am *that*"—meaning an object. "I just am." "You are what?"—"I am that I am."So, beyond "I am" no words can possibly be of any use. That is what it means.

## 9. Acceptance, Witnessing and Understanding— three different words for the same "I-Am"

Q: *After waking up in the morning somehow it is known that I had a good or bad sleep, although I wasn't aware of sleeping. I wasn't there during sleep. Nothing was there during sleep. And still, on waking up one knows how one slept. Therefore, something must have been present during sleep that could record the nature of one's sleep. What is there in deep sleep and how does one's sleep get remembered on waking up as soon as the "I-Am" arises?*

A: That which exists all the time is what remembers the sleep: the "I-Am." It is the impersonal Consciousness, the impersonal sense of awareness. What was absent in deep sleep? The personal identification was absent. However, the "I-Am" is always present. "I am Madhukar" was absent. That's why Madhukar did not know that he had a good sleep.

On waking up, the identified consciousness comes into being as "I am Madhukar." And it is through the impersonal Consciousness, "I-Am," that the personal consciousness "I am Madhukar" comes to know that there was good sleep.

Ramana Maharshi and almost every advocate of *Advaita* explain this point of the teaching quite often. They say what I say: in addition to the individual identified consciousness, there is something else present at all times in all men and in everything that exists. It is the impersonal Consciousness which enables a human being to say, "I know this or I don't know that." You can only know something or not know something when you are conscious. To know or not know something, Consciousness needs to be present; not the identified consciousness, but the pure impersonal Consciousness. It is because of the pure Knowing-ness, "I-Am," that an individual can say, "I know or I do not know."

Q: *Is the "I-Am" what is called the witness?*

A: That is correct, Madhukar. "I-Am" is the understanding. "I-Am" is the understanding that results when there is acceptance. And "I -Am" is the understanding that transforms itself into witnessing.

## 10. The Ability to Foresee the Future is not a Necessary Condition for Being a Sage

Q: *This is a personal question regarding you.*

A: OK. I meant to tell you earlier what I have somehow omitted to say specifically so far: you are free to ask any personal questions. However, if a question is totally irrelevant to the teaching, then I may say so and not answer it. For instance, if you ask me, "How many times do you have sex with your wife?", I will probably tell you that it is none of your business. That means your question and my possible answer are irrelevant for our discussions. Short of such matters, you are free to ask any personal question. I understand your curiosity about my personal life. There can be genuine questions about it. Go ahead and ask your question.

Q: *You say the past, the present and the future are already there. Although realization may have happened to them, it seems that few sages actually know the future, or their past lives. In your case, do you know the future and/or your past lives?*

A: I can only speak about my case. I cannot tell you what happens in other enlightened cases. I am told that Ramana Maharshi could understand what the birds and animals were saying or thinking within their limited ego. Apparently there is a story regarding a bird, a sparrow who flew into the room and twittered something. Ramana is supposed to have told his attendant in this particular case: "This sparrow is complaining that you destroyed his nest." Perhaps, he was only making fun of his assistant because Ramana Maharshi is, like many other sages, known for his tremendous sense of humor. But perhaps what he said to the attendant was exactly what had happened. Or, perhaps there was such a great transparency between the bird and the sage that such a direct communication was possible between them without needing any human interpretation.

However, the mind will say, "How could Ramana know the language of the bird? Does he know bird language? How can a human being and a bird understand each other or speak the same language?" All these are lateral questions posed by the mind.

What I am trying to say is that certain powers may manifest with the event of enlightenment. In fact, Ramana Maharshi was once asked, "Is the arising of *kundalini* a necessary precedent for the occurrence of enlightenment?" He answered very clearly, "No, *kundalini* may arise or it may not arise. But its arising is definitely not a necessary condition for enlightenment to happen." As I said, certain psychic or other powers may manifest in an enlightened one. But these powers are not deliberately, volitionally, exercised by the sage.

Let me tell you another story about Ramana Maharshi: a woman came to him with a dead child and asked him to bring it back to life. The Maharshi did not say anything. The child remained dead. After she had gone, someone asked him, "Bhagavan, why didn't you revive the child?" His answer was, "There was no *sankalpa*." *Sankalpa* means intention. The only meaning I attach to his saying "There was no intention" is that if there had been an intention on Bhagavan's part, the child might have come to life again. But it was not the child's destiny to be revived.

There are innumerable cases in which sages have revived dead bodies. My interpretation is that it is the destiny of a person to have death postponed. A revival will only happen if it is destined, otherwise it won't.

There are sages who can certainly look into the future. What is more important for me is the fact that there are many people who, without being sages, can also look into the future. Being able to look into the future is not a necessary condition for being a sage.

## 11. Consciousness is Snapping the Chain of Thinking

Q: *Ramana speaks quite often of the effortless, thought-free state. Is the effortless, thought-free state what is called enlightenment?*

A: Yes. The effortless, thought-free state... Let us first ask, "Who is making the effort? Who does the thinking?"

Q: *It's the "me."*

A: Yes, it is the individual, the "me." The presence of understanding cannot happen along with the presence of a "me." Enlightenment or the presence of understanding can happen only in the absence of the "me." That is what Ramana means with the effortless, thought-free state.

Q: *Do you mean to say that in that state thinking can happen, but that there is no "me" involved in it?*

A: I make a notional distinction between thought and thinking. I must repeat: what I say here is a concept, but it's a useful concept. Ramana Maharshi did not use the word "thinking." Because presumably he did not say the word "thinking" in English, he must have used the equivalent word in his native language Tamil. However what he said in this context has been correctly translated as "thinking." Ramana said, "Thinking is not man's real nature, but the arising of the thought is not within his control." His words mean that the arising of thoughts, of desires and of emotions can and do happen even after enlightenment. Why? Because the brain exists in a sage as well as in an ordinary person. Because the brain is merely a receiving apparatus, thoughts arise in both the sage and the non-sage. However, what happens in the case of sage when a thought arises? The sage merely witnesses the thought. When a thought is

135

merely witnessed, it is not taken delivery of. That means the thought which has arisen is not pursued and no further thinking occurs. In the ordinary person further involved thinking happens when a thought is pursued. Thinking is involvement. We could say that a thought is what starts the thinking. But not every thought leads to thinking.

Q: *Could you explain what Ramana means with his words "The snapping of the chain"?*

A: The snapping of the chain of thoughts occurs at the moment when witnessing begins. Suppose a thought arises and you get involved in it and thinking occurs. During the involvement in thinking, a sudden snapping of the thinking chain can occur in the sudden realization that I am unnecessarily involved in a thinking process. That sudden realization and the snapping of the chain of thinking are not part of the thinking mechanism and process. That sudden snapping of the thinking comes about from a totally different dimension. It is the understanding or Consciousness that is snapping the chain. Then witnessing happens.

In other words, what I mean to say is that you start the thinking. You start the involvement. You cannot break the chain of thoughts and thinking. It can only be broken when there is a certain amount of understanding.

That is why I say, "Do not underestimate or discount

intellectual understanding." Understanding in most cases begins on the intellectual level. But the intellectual understanding will lead, at a certain point, to the snapping of the chain of thinking.

## 12. Has Man the Freedom to Inquire Who He Is?

Q: *I read in one of Ramana's books: "The only freedom man has is to inquire and to find out who he really is." My question is: what freedom does the human being have, if whatever happens is God's Will? As I understand it, I don't think that this quotation expresses Ramana's final teaching.*

A: No. I don't think so either.

Q: *Perhaps this teaching was meant for a specific seeker who needed to hear it at that point in his search.*

A: That is correct. Ramana must have talked to a particular person regarding his situation at a given time. I cannot imagine that Ramana Maharshi would be teaching a tenet like that. He was once asked, "If I raise my hand, is it because of my free will, or is because it is predetermined?" Ramana's answer to this question was very clear. He said, "The raising of your arm happens according to predetermined plans." Perhaps in the quote you have cited, Ramana was misunderstood, or the translation of his words was not accurate or correct.

## 13. Nothing Ever Really Happened or Will Happen

Q: *You quoted Ramana this morning as having said that even lifting an arm is destined.*

A: Yes. Predestination is definitely Ramana's position. I think that particular question was asked by Arthur Osborne.

Q: *From what Ramana is saying, it follows that whatever happens at this moment is also destined.*

A: Absolutely.

Q: *And whatever happened in the past was also destined.*

A: Absolutely.

Q: *And whatever will happen in the future is also destined*

A: Yes, absolutely.

Q: *It could therefore be destined that this body-mind organism called "Madhukar" may disappear unenlightened and another future organism will instead get enlightened at some other time and place. According to you all of this is already predestined.*

A: Yes, absolutely, all that is definitely predestined.

Q: *From the point of view of total predestination, there wouldn't be any room whatsoever for evolution. Because whatever will happen, exists already and only "waits" to be delivered at the right place and time in the history of a person or in that of the universe.*

A: That is absolutely correct. And that is what Ramana Maharshi means with his words "There is no creation and there is no dissolution." Precisely in this sense, nothing ever happened and nothing will ever happen.

## 14. "You" Cannot Create a Thought

Q: *You teach that a thought comes from outside, and is received by the brain. Thinking then happens inside, within the brain. An arising thought triggers further thinking. For instance the thought "money" will trigger further thoughts on money.*

A: That is correct

Q: *The thought which is received from what you call "outside" is being received inside the brain, so to speak. My question is why do you speak of inside and outside? For me there is no inside and outside. The first thought and the thoughts that follow it, can be seen as initiated from within or from without. It is merely a question of the way we want to see it. Furthermore, if everything is Consciousness and if whatever happens or is thought of is predestined, it doesn't really matter where thought and thinking occur, or where they are produced or come from.*

A: No, no. Wait a minute! As an example, let us take the thought about money. At a certain moment, the thought about money has occurred. The thought about money occurred, but not the thought about a woman. The thought about food didn't occur either nor any other thought about anything else. As soon as the thought about money occurred, the brain reacted to it and involved thinking took place. Therefore, you have no control over this original thought about money that came in. That is my point.

Q: *Do you mean to say it doesn't matter where thought comes from—from the outside or inside?*

A: No, no. The question really is, did you create that thought? Did your brain create that thought? Or did the thought arise for your brain to react to it? I am saying that you cannot create a thought. The brain cannot create a thought. The brain can only react to a thought. That is why I distinguish between a thought and thinking. Thinking is created by the brain. But the original thought that leads to that thinking is not created by the brain. And what kind of thought may occur is not in your hands.

Mind you, a thought about money was quite

unlikely to have occurred to a brain of a body-mind organism called Einstein. The thoughts of an Albert Einstein would naturally be thoughts about his work and related matters.

## 15. Who Is Ramesh?—Who Are You?

Q: *Friends of mine have asked me several times: who is Ramesh? I ask you: "Who are you?" What would you answer to my friends?*

A: "Who are you?" and "Who is Ramesh?" are two different questions. Who or what is Ramesh? Ramesh is the name given to a body-mind organism. Even if the name is changed, the organism will still remain the same. No matter what name the organism has, that which functions through it and through any other organism, is Consciousness.

Therefore, if you mean to ask, "Who is Ramesh?" or "Who is Madhukar?" or "Who is Thomas?", the answer is: "All of them are the objective expression of the same impersonal, universal, cosmic Consciousness." That is the answer.

Who or what is functioning? "I-I" or the universal Consciousness or God. Through what is Consciousness functioning? Through the instrument called Ramesh, Thomas or Madhukar. That is the answer.

## 16. Why do You Hang up Ramana's Picture and not Maharaj's?

Q: *I see Ramana Maharshi's picture hanging up there just behind you. I was wondering last night why you don't have a picture of your guru Nisargdatta Maharaj up as well? What is the reason behind that? Is there any?*

A: The reason is that my earliest inspiration came from Ramana Maharshi. Therefore I honor him very much. The more practical reason is that I don't have a photograph of Maharaj which is big enough to be hung up there.

## 17. "I Remember my sleep, although 'I' was not there when it occurred. How come?"

Q: *During deep sleep there is no awareness of the fact that one is sleeping.*

A: That is correct.

Q: *However, on waking up, there is the memory of the fact that one has slept. It seems that memory must have somehow recorded one's sleeping. Is there a kind of transfer from the "nothing" of deep sleep to memory, and from memory to the brain of the waking body-mind organism?*

A: No. However there is a shift from the impersonality

to the personality, and from disidentification to identification when we wake up from sleep.

Q: *Does that happen during the "nothing" of deep sleep or does that happen at a moment in time—a second or so after waking up?*

A: No. Time doesn't exist in deep sleep. Only after waking up, you say, "I slept for six hours."

Q: *The memory seems to know it. When we say, "I slept six hours," do we speak from the past? Can we say that because we remember it?*

A: Yes.

Q: *How is memory able to "catch" the fact that sleep has happened during the unconscious time. How can there be memory without consciousness?*

A: Oh, there was Conscousness! That is the whole point, Madhukar. Consciousness had to be there during sleep. Otherwise, how would you know that you had a good sleep or disturbed sleep? Something had to be present because of which—on waking up—you are able to state, "I slept well or I didn't sleep well."

However, identified consciousness was absent during deep sleep. What was present in deep sleep? It was the impersonal cosmic Consciousness.

Q: *Is memory part of the unidentified Consciousness as well as of the identified consciousness?*

A: Everything is part of Consciousness. Consciousness is all there is. There is nothing other than Consciousness. Memory is Consciousness. Consciousness is everything there is. Consciousness is the very foundation of all phenomenality.

## 18. Listening and Talking Happen—"You" Are Doing Nothing

Q: *As I see it, what we are doing here is trying to understand the Truth intellectually by discussing your teaching. What you say seems to be quite clear. I understand it all well. But what happens is actually beyond this bouncing back and forth ideas, questions and answers. It transcends all talks and discussions. I can somehow feel or intuit the transcendence happening beneath the words. When an answer is given, it is not the answer that remains but the transcendent silence. However, for me, that transcendence is a feeling that comes and goes rather than a permanent existential actuality. Do you know what I mean?*

A: Yes, I do.

Q: *Although I would love to be eternally in "That," I know that I can do nothing to make it happen. In me, there is this immense longing. That's the only thing that seems to be staying with me permanently. That's all there is that's permanent in my case: the longing.*

A: You began your sentence with the answer. The answer to your question is contained in what you said at the very outset of your speaking. You began your sentence by saying, "What we are doing here is…" And you continued to say whatever you then said. I want to point out that there is nothing you can do here, there or anywhere. What is happening here is that there are some people doing the listening to the talking that is taking place. What "you" are doing is nothing. The listening is taking place as part of the impersonal functioning of Totality. And what this event—the talking and listening are one event—will produce in the functioning of Totality, only Totality knows.

"I am here listening to you with the idea that I shall get something out of it," is a wrong notion. Until that basic misconceived idea dissolves, the transcendence, the inference from Consciousness cannot happen. That can only happen if you listen without the following attitudes: "I am listening and I don't understand it"; or "I intellectually understand it, but I am not able to go deeper into it"; or "How do I go deeper; what should I do for the intellectual understanding to go deeper?" These kind of attitudes are the biggest obstruction to understanding.

Q: *Are you saying that everything that happens here at this moment is just happening as the What-is? It is as it is, and that's all there is to it?*

A: That's right. That's all there is. At the present moment, that's all there is.

Q: *I understand what you are saying. Understanding what you teach, however, hasn't stopped the deep feeling of longing for final peace in me. That's how it is and that's the What-is for the body-mind organism called Madhukar.*

A: As long as the longing exists, the final transcendence cannot happen. And I quite agree with you: your longing is part of What-is. Of course, it is the What-is. I understand your frustration, Madhukar.

The whole problem is that the individual wants something—and I have repeated this any number of times. Whether the wanting is for something material or spiritual makes no difference. The fact remains that there is a person who wants something—there is a wanting and there is the wanted object. There is someone who wants something that is wanted, and there is the process of wanting. As long as that triad remains, the transcendence cannot happen.

At some point you perhaps will accept the situation which includes your wanting, the longing and the frustration. This situation is indeed part of What-is. The frustration has got to be accepted and faced. But the mind may say, "I am frustrated, I don't want to be frustrated."

## 19. Judging and Comparing is the Disease of the Mind

Q: *There are different types of gurus. Some may be genuine and some may be false. Life consists of both good and bad; of people like Mother Teresa and like Hitler. Phenomenality consists of all opposites. To be a bad person or a false guru is therefore nobody's fault, because both and anything else are part of the impersonal What-is. All and everything are part of God's Will and could therefore not be otherwise.*

A: That's correct.

Q: *If a seeker meets with an incomplete guru, that is exactly what needs to happen to him. That's why it happens.*

A: That's correct.

Q: *In the cosmic picture there is no "false" and no "genuine."*

A: That is again correct.

Q: *To speak about false gurus and discuss their false teachings is therefore futile because we would question the Will of God, right?*

A: That would be unnecessary involvement. What you have said is quite correct: whatever happens at any moment is part of the functioning of Totality. A false guru is part of What-is. It is only the mind that compares and judges. Let me tell you the beautiful statement of a Chinese sage: "To distinguish between what you like and what you don't like is the disease of the mind."

In other words, comparing and judging is a disease of the mind. And if that happens, it is also a part of What-is. When the understanding goes deeper, the Chinese sage's saying will always remain at the back of your mind.

## 20. A Disciple's Enlightenment: Encouragement for His Co-disciples and Proof of the Guru's Power

Q: *I can easily recognize you as an enlightened guru and master. On the other hand, it is important to me as a seeker to know if your guruship has "produced" one or more disciples of yours who have blossomed into the same complete level of enlightened understanding that you have. To know of the occurrence of enlightenment in one or some of your devotees would definitely give me great courage to keep my own search going. And it would give me hope to end it possibly successfully. Therefore my question is, "Are there any of your devotees who have the same understanding you have? Do any enlightened devotees of yours exist?"*

A: Do you want me to specify and name some people?

Q: *Well, you can go all the way and name them.*

A: There have been some and there are some, yes. What Henry (Swift) told you yesterday should give you an indication of what has been happening regarding my devotees' enlightenment. *(The day before, Ramesh had asked Henry Swift to tell those present at the seminar about his spiritual search and how it had ended.[1])* In his report, Henry made it perfectly clear that he remained a perfectly ordinary gentleman after enlightenment—like me.

For something to happen, for enlightenment to happen, the instrument—the body-mind organism—has to be ready. And when the instrument is ready, enlightenment can happen from any level, from the intellectual level or any other level.

So, if you mean to ask whether there have been cases in which the understanding has been total, and enlightenment has happened, my answer is yes. In more than one case? Yes! In how many cases? I don't know.

---

[1] For an account of Henry Swift's enlightenment see *Enlightenment: An Outbreak*, Chapter 2 (Neti Neti Press, Pune, India, 1998)

## 21. In Therapy, You are Responsible for your Deeds—In Spirituality, All Deeds are God's Deeds

Q: *Could you explain the aspect of personal responsibility in therapy and how that concept fits into your teaching?*

A: Henning, would you talk about this subject for us?

Henning: *OK, I will try. Ramesh, you and me, we had a discussion about this subject in Munich some years ago—do you remember? When I had met you at the time in Munich, I did not understand your teaching yet. But in the meantime I found out through your teaching that all actions in the entire universe are God's actions. And therefore also His responsibility.*

*At the beginning of my work with patients, I make it really clear to them that they are really responsible, personally, for what happens with them. That's a very important point in my work.*

*Let me sum up my experience as a therapist: in my work, I am hesitating to tell my clients the whole truth of the teaching—namely, that whatever happens is according to God's Will. At the beginning of their therapeutic work, the clients shouldn't be told the basic truth of your teaching. I tell them, sternly and strictly, that they should be responsible for what they are experiencing. This is very important. If they are not told so, they will never get well.*

A: Quite right. But after your clients have taken on

personal responsibility, does their life change?

Henning: *Oh, definitely yes! Usually it doesn't take long for them to take on responsibilities. And then it might take only a few days more until they go further.*

A: So, an old pattern of behavior is a sort of wooden printing block which comes into operation each time a certain life situation occurs. And taking responsibility is like shedding a certain printing block from one's life, isn't it?

Henning: *Yes, one could say that. That's the most important part of my work. I have learned from my therapy work that some clients have spiritual experiences from the very beginning. Others are slower. But any experience has to be dealt with as it comes up. If somebody has a spiritual experience in the very first hour of his or her very first breathing session, the therapist should not say, "Stop it, you haven't felt your pain yet!" It is much better to work with what is sound and healthy in a client than to work with what is unhealthy. Healing happens faster and goes deeper if we use the healthy part of the client. On the other hand, if we are trying to discover even the last bit of unhealthiness in a person, therapy will go on for many years.*

A: Quite so.

Henning: *But if we enable the person to open up to his very*

151

*nature right from the beginning, therapy takes very little time. Sometimes just a few days.*

### 22. The Silence of the Absence of the Thinking Mind teaches You what You Really Are

Q: *Many teachers, including the Maharshi, teach that silence is very helpful to spiritual realization. We don't have any silent periods during the seminar, nor do we speak much about silence here. Can silence be a technique or sadhana? Could you say something about this subject? Is the state of disidentification a state of silence?*

A: I think Henning will tell you something about silence. I heard that silence is part of the EST technique.

Henning: *No, it is not.*

A: I heard about EST's technique: it uses and involves a constant stream of questions and answers. And suddenly the leader of the group says, "Stop!" At that moment all talking freezes in an instant. Everybody stops talking abruptly. At this moment, the participants notice the state they were in. In the ensuing silence, the "me" is absent. This is what the technique does. When mental activity stops abruptly there is silence. And in that silence—when the "me" and the thinking are absent—you are in your true nature.

Q: *I understand what you are saying. Isn't permanent silence enlightenment? I have heard it defined in this way by several teachers. I believe that is why the "me" desires permanent silence. But wanting silence is still the same game of seeking, isn't it?*

A: Not talking is not silence. There is silence when the mind is no longer active. When the thinking mind is absent, silence is. The silence of the absence of the thinking mind teaches you what you are. In fact, you know your real nature only in that silence, in that present moment, when the mind is totally inert. It is in this way that silence helps you in your understanding.

The real teaching is in silence, because in silence nobody has to tell you anything. Nobody can tell you anything. When the mind is not active at all, you are already what you really are, That is how I interpret the word silence.

Q: *During a moment of silence, there is silence plus consciousness as pure Witnessing.*

A: That is correct. The same Consciousness which prevails in silence, prevails also in the state of deep sleep. Silence and deep sleep continue until the silent state is disturbed when the mind begins its activity or sleep comes to an end on waking up. The mind starts its activity again as the identified consciousness, the individual mind.

Q: *There is no way to produce silence, or is there?*

A: No. That's exactly the point. There is no way to produce this. Because the one who wants to produce this silence is the "me." The active mind wants to produce silence. Silence is the state in which the wanting mind and the intellect are absent.

## 23. Thinking Mind, Working Mind, Intellect and Ego

Q: *Is the thinking mind the ego?*

A: The thinking mind is the ego.

Q: *Could the working mind be also called the intellect?*

A: No, the thinking mind is the intellect. Thinking mind and intellect go together. The working mind is only concerned with what happens spontaneously, or with spontaneous action.

Q: *It belongs actually to the action itself.*

A: That is correct. It belongs to the action itself, really.

## 24. When Frustration Leads to Prayer, You have Entered the Dark Night of the Soul

Q: *I heard you say that the search for enlightenment starts with the individual. In my own case, it occurred at some point that my search turned into a prayer. It has become a prayer with the objective that the "me" may be "taken in."*

A: That can happen. That is part of the process of dis-identification. Frustration can arise at any stage of the process.

Q: The search changes from doing *sadhana* to simply praying.

A: It could lead to anything. Of course, it can lead to prayer.

Q: *Is praying still a doing? Praying is definitely still wanting something.*

A: Yes. When frustration leads to prayer, you have entered what they call the dark night of the soul. Then an outside intervention or outside interference may occur.

Q: *And that is all in the plan.*

A: That's how it is. It's all in the plan.

# Part 3

# Silent Arrow

*The Search for God-Truth-Reality;*
Article by Ramesh S. Balsekar published
in "The Mountain Path," December, 1991

Ramesh in his study; January 1999

Ramesh first came to know of Nisargadatta Maharaj—the master who was to be his *satguru*—by reading Jean Dunn's article about Maharaj in the October 1978 issue of *The Mountain Path,* a spiritual journal which is published biannually by the Sri Ramanashramam, Tiruvannamalai, India. As part of my interest in Ramesh's teachings, I was prompted to try and track down any material that he had published, and I wondered whether he himself had ever written anything for *The Mountain Path.* When I first asked Ramesh about this, he answered in the negative, but then in spring 1996, an American seeker came up from Tiruvanna-malai to meet Ramesh in Bombay. He claimed to have read an article by Ramesh in *The Mountain Path* while at the Sri Ramanashram a few days earlier. Ramesh then remembered writing the article, and I was able to trace it to the December 1991 issue of the magazine. Its direct and comprehensive expression of his teaching provides a fitting end to this book.

# Introductory Note

The following article by Ramesh S. Balsekar was published in the December 1991 issue of *The Mountain Path* (Volume 28, Nos. 3 and 4, pp 129-134). It is reprinted here, unabridged, by kind permission of the Sri Ramanashramam. Writing with great clarity and elegance, Ramesh manages to condense his teachings into a few pages. In contrast to the preceding sections which consist of excerpts and fragments drawn from Ramesh's responses to, and interactions with, his audience, the teachings in this part come straight from his own pen and heart.

Instead of being worked over by incessant hammer blows, or cut down by the precise, almost surgical, strokes of his sword, we find ourselves somehow in Ramesh's presence as we read. His words flow on smoothly, stirring no questioning ripples in the mind. The separation between the guru and the disciple dissolves. Like a silent arrow, the teaching strikes home. His teaching becomes the understanding, and that understanding is what we are. And as we put the book down, we remain as that which we truly are—that which prevails prior even to silence. The arrow has hit the Heart.

# 1. Man's Search for Security

The individual's search for God begins from the time he realizes, when dealing with life's problems, the strict limitation of his puny intellect and of his supposed free will. He then turns to that Supreme Power—God— and prays for material things in this world to satisfy what in the beginning he considered to be his needs. An animal's search is normally restricted to the satisfaction of its biological needs, but the search of the human being extends beyond his immediate needs. Man cannot enjoy the present without a reasonable guarantee that his satisfaction will be extended into the foreseeable future. And it is this aspect which turns his need into greed; before he knows it, this accumulative tendency has become an obsession, long after the foreseeable future has been adequately taken care of.

Man's search for security is based on the mistaken belief that there can be something constant and unchanging in this world. The fact of the matter, however, is that nothing in this universe is constant: every planet and every galaxy is in continual movement; every living organism is a mass of cells, continually being created, destroyed and recreated in a specific pattern of vibrating energy. Life itself is a series of changes between opposites. Life means living, living means continual change, and change inevitably means insecurity. The search for security has made life for most people a matter—a confirmed habit—of either looking behind or thinking of the fears and hopes ahead. These fluctuating perspectives render illusory the reality of What-is—the here and now.

We seem to forget that music is such a delight only because of its flow and rhythm, and that the very basis of that delight would be destroyed if we were to prolong a particular note or chord beyond its legitimate time merely because we liked it and would like to hear more of it. Life, like music, is a flowing process, and we would make life an impossible conflict (and many of us have indeed accomplished this!) if we were to arrest its normal flow because we liked certain parts and feared others. It is impossible to be blind to the fact that, in spite of the best-laid plans, illness must occur and accidents must happen. Because these unpredictable events, or others like them, are inevitable, there can thus be no solution to the problem of fear of an uncertain future which is based on the premise that permanence and security are attainable through personal effort. There can only be a dissolution of the problem through a bold and clear look not at it, but into it, with no separation of the "me" from the problem.

## 2. The Separation of the Individual From the Totality of the Universe

Basically, the fear of change and uncertainty arises because of the separation of the individual "me" from the rest of the universe—the separation of the individual from Totality—and this fear can disappear only when this separation gets bridged through the realization that the "me" itself is an illusion. The truth of the matter is that we are struggling ceaselessly to ensure the continuity, permanence and security of this "me"—the apparent thinker of our thoughts, the experiencer of our experiences, the knower of our knowledge—without realizing that it is essentially nothing but an illusion.

An awareness of the illusion of "me" can arise only with the realization that our experience as such, whatever its nature, must necessarily be in the present moment. In the actual experience of the present moment, there is no experiencer, for the "me" as the experiencer arises only when the mind recreates the experience. The notion of "me," as distinct from the experience, comes only from memory and from the rapidity with which thoughts occur. It is, as Nisargadatta Maharaj used to say, like a burning stick whirling in the air giving the illusion of a continuous circle of fire and light.

"I feel happy" simply means that a feeling of happiness is present; "I am afraid" simply means that fear is present. To understand this is to realize that life can really be lived only in the present moment—here and now—that there can be neither security nor permanence in life, that both are as much of a myth, an illusion, as is the "me" that demands to be protected.

Every experience is in some sense new and fresh, and at every moment of our lives we are in the midst of the new and unknown. We can clearly realize this when the experience of the moment is accepted without resisting it, without giving it a label based on past memory. Peace and happiness consist in being completely open and sensitive to the experience of the moment, with the deepest conviction that it is in complete accordance with God's Will, or, if you prefer to express it differently, with the functioning of Totality. Accept the experience of the moment, and let it die with the moment. The secret of life is to understand that the past must be abandoned, that the unknown cannot be avoided, and that nothing in the world can be definitely known and fixed. This, incidentally, is precisely the conclusion which quantum physics has arrived at. As Goethe has put it, "As long as you do not know how to die and come to life again, you are but a sorry traveller on this dark earth."

## 3. Man's Search for Truth, or God

At some stage in his incessant search for security, the human being realizes that there really cannot be any genuine security in this world, that the search for reality is truly an exercise in futility and frustration, and indeed, that material success in life cannot really bring peace and happiness. At this juncture, the mind turns inward, and the nature of the search changes from looking for material success and future security to Self-inquiry, or it manifests as a desire to be one with God. In this attempt to find out "what it is all about," the spiritual seeker is born.

Spiritual seeking begins with the individual wanting, as an individual, the supreme "bliss" that is usually promised and held out as a bait to the seeker. The seeking can only really end, though, with the annihilation of the individual seeker and the realization that the individual is only an instrument for the impersonal working of Totality, an instrument of God's inscrutable ways. During the period between the beginning of the spiritual search by the individual and the ultimate realization that the individual truly has no personal free will and therefore cannot make any effort, the poor miserable seeker goes through various kinds of therapies, disciplines and maneuvers prescribed by various paths and sects. This occurs because he is firmly entrenched in the belief that the success of his search depends wholly on the efforts that he makes and the determination with which he makes the efforts. The untold misery and frustration of this kind of seeking only comes to an end when the seeker understands that the success or failure of his search is in the hands of the Totality, or God. Only when the sudden realization dawns that nothing genuine can be "achieved" by any individual, will the surrender of the individual free will occur. The heart will then be open and receptive to the Grace of God or Totality.

When the Totality appears within, the Totality without is simultaneously revealed. Some have called it God-realization; others have called it liberation, enlightenment, *moksha*. The one thing common to all these expressions is the fact that the individual, as an independent doer, has disappeared.

Reality seems extraordinary, something very special, only because of the individual seeker's expectations. When it is actually experienced, there is a sudden realization that nothing extraordinary has really happened. There is just an understanding that the abnormal aberration of the "me" has disappeared, and there exists in its place only the very normal What-is. The "What-is" is the *sahaja sthiti*, the natural state of phenomenality. It is original, ordinary, natural, normal, witnessed by the whole mind, not tainted by the split mind of the involved human being that views all things from the divisive viewpoint of subject-object.

The individual, in "his" search for enlightenment, has to face various problems created by his split mind. One of these is: What is the best path for spiritual seeking? Similarly, another problem is: Is *sadhana* necessary for achieving the spiritual goal? If so, what is the best *sadhana*? If not, why is it that there are so many spiritual paths that insist on a particular *sadhana*?

The fact of the matter is that nature provides astonishingly clear indications of one's *dharma* in one's own body-mind organism. Each body-mind organism, at the moment of conception, is "stamped" with certain natural characteristics—physical, mental, temperamental—which make up the personality of the individual organism. This set of natural characteristics gives a remarkable indication of the trends in life which the organism will be inclined to follow, and to that extent may be considered as indicating its *dharma*. Thus, by and large, it is possible to see even in the early years of an individual, the trends and indications of what he is likely to become as an individual person, what his broad profession or occupation is likely to be, and indeed, what spiritual path he is likely to take to! This is a bold and unusual assertion which I shall attempt to substantiate in the next section.

## 4. What is the Best Path for Me?

It is rather interesting that Dr. William Sheldon and his associate worked out, in the 1930's, a remarkably comprehensive and well-developed system which classifies all human beings. Dr. Sheldon's classification is based on the premise that each individual is an amalgam in varying proportions of three physical and three correlated psychological elements. The three components are fairly evenly blended in most people to make a generally complex character, but the fact remains that the classification can be created on the basis of the disparate characteristics.

The term *dharma*, used so effectively in the *Bhagvad Gita*, denotes the cardinal characteristics, the innate nature of the sentient being, and is considered to be the basis of his very being, his active life. Dr. Sheldon's classification is a modern attempt to classify human beings on the basis of their physical, emotional and mental characteristics. Broadly speaking, his classification is as follows:

a) *Endomorph-Visceratonic*: the essential physical characteristic is a soft roundness built around the digestive tract, with a corresponding temperamental pattern based on love of food, comfort and luxury— a type that projects an indiscriminate extroversion and emotionality that makes him prone to a craving for affection not only from the closest family members but also from the whole world. Consequently, he loves the whole world!

b) *Mesomorph-Somatotonic*: physically big-boned with hard and strong muscles, correlated to a temperament that is depicted by an intense love for physical activity and restlessness, an aggressive and almost uncontrolled lust for power, an unusual capacity to bear pain, coupled with occasional shocking insensitivity towards the feelings of others. There is a strong competitive instinct, which is coupled with uncommon physical endurance, courage and intrepidity. The somatotonic prefers to bear his pains and travails in solitude.

c) *Estomorph-Cerebrotonic:* physically slender with small bones and weak muscles, with a temperament characterized by an over-sensitivity coupled with an over-alertness of the brain. The confirmed cerebrotonic is an incorrigible introvert, concerned more with what is behind the apparent scene than the scene itself, concerned more with the essential core than the apparent matter. He is quite content to be allowed to lead his own life peacefully, and is not concerned with power and domination over others or with competitive affairs.

This analysis lends itself smoothly and easily to the three paths of salvation contained in the Hindu tradition. The visceratonic's natural propensity towards externalizing his emotions would make him almost automatically take the path of devotion to a personal God (*bhakti*) with its inherent component of universal goodwill accompanied by charity and compassion towards all sentient beings. The path of action (*karma*) would obviously suit the somatotonic with an abundance of physical stamina and energy which makes him "on the go" all the time. Similarly, the path of knowledge (*jnana*) would be clearly marked out for the introverted cerebrotonic.

Many of the problems confronting the seeker would disappear if he would only remember that spiritual seeking itself started as a matter of Grace; that he did not choose voluntarily to be a seeker. The fact that the search for security and material prosperity suddenly gave way to a search for Truth should be acknowledged to be a manifestation of divine Grace. It is this Grace which directs the seeker's path and guides him along it.

## 5. Is Effort as *Sadhana* Necessary?

The essential point to be remembered about individual effort—*sadhana*—is that a certain amount of disciplinary practice is necessary in the beginning to still the mind. This new type of seeking that has been redirected from the search outside towards the search inside needs to be nurtured. The nature of such a disciplinary practice is that the practice may eventually become so interesting that one forgets that it is only a means to an end. The practitioner must eventually disappear in the impersonal goal, but when this is forgotten, the means often becomes an end in itself. Thus, in the matter of meditation, the purpose of meditation is conveniently forgotten, and an element of competition sometimes develops among its practitioners concerning the length of each other's meditation and the "benefits" (which are really nothing but the projections of the mind) which the seeker has been able to "achieve."

It is most pertinent to listen to Ramana Maharshi when he says:

1) "Light-gazing stupefies the mind and produces catalepsy of the will for the time being, and it secures no permanent benefit (result). Breath-control temporarily benumbs the will, but it is not permanent. It is the same with listening to sounds, unless the *mantra* is sacred and secures the help of the higher Power to purify and raise the thoughts."

2) "Unbroken 'I-I' is the infinite ocean. The ego, the 'I'-thought, remains only a bubble on it and is called *jiva* or individual soul. The bubble too is water, for when it bursts it only mixes in the ocean. When it remains a bubble it is still a part of the ocean. Ignorant of this simple truth, innumerable methods under different denominations, such as *yoga, bhakti, karma*, each again with many modifications, are being taught with great skill and in intricate detail only to entice the seekers and confuse their minds. So also are the religions and sects and dogmas."

3) "He who instructs an ardent seeker to do this or that is not a true master. The seeker is already afflicted by his activities and wants peace and rest. In other words, he wants cessation of his activities. If the teacher tells him to do something in addition to, or in place of, his other activities, can that be a help to the seeker?

"Activity is creation. Activity is the destruction of one's inherent happiness. If activity is advocated, the adviser is not a master but a killer. Such a person cannot liberate the aspirant, he can only strengthen his fetters."

It will also be instructive to listen to Bayazid of Bistun, who has given the course of his spiritual journey in his confessions:

"For twelve years I was the smith of my soul. I put it in the furnace of austerity and burnt it in the fire of combat. I laid it on the anvil of reproach and smote it with the hammer of blame until I made of my soul a mirror. Five years I was the mirror of myself and was ever polishing that mirror with diverse acts of worship and piety. On my waist I wore a girdle of pride and vanity, and self-conceit and reliance on devotion and approbation of my works. I labored for five years until that girdle became worn out and I professed Islam anew. I looked and saw that all created things were dead: I pronounced four *takbirs* (prayers) over them and returned from the funeral of all of them and, without intrusion of creatures, through God's help alone, I attained unto God."

Thus the spiritual search begins with the individual seeking enlightenment as a means to peace and happiness. The search can end only when there is the sudden awakening to the realization that the seeking itself is the massive obstruction to enlightenment. So long as there is a "me" as an individual entity, a doer, wanting something—even if that something be called enlightenment or God—the great awakening cannot happen. When the great awakening happens, it is the great magnificent leap into impersonality, where there is no "one" left to inquire what has happened to whom.

The fact of the matter is that in the phenomenal flow of space-time, there is a continuous process of evolution in all fields—art, music, science, spirituality. Spiritual seeking is an impersonal, evolutionary process proceeding through various psychosomatic organisms, each with varying inherent characteristics, until an organism is conceived and created with adequate capacity to receive the Truth through intuitive, subjective experience. It is necessary to understand that this evolutionary process has used very many different human organisms, many different lives in many births, before it has created a highly evolved organism and, more importantly, that they are not "re-births" of the same soul or ego. The human organisms are merely instruments through which the evolutionary process happens. Enlightenment can only happen as an impersonal happening—no individual psychosomatic apparatus can become enlightened.

It would, perhaps, be fitting to conclude this essay with a quotation attributed to the Buddha:

> "As there is no self, there is no transmigration of self, but there are deeds and continued effects of deeds. There are deeds being done, but there is no doer. There is no entity that migrates, no self is transferred from one place to another; but there is a voice uttered here and the echo of it comes back."

And, of course, it is very necessary to bear constantly in mind the final truth, as pronounced by Ramana Maharshi, that there is really no creation, no destruction; no free will, no destiny; no path, no achievement.

# Glossary

Advaita

>    Non-duality. (*a*=negative particle + *dvaita*=duality)
>    The most important branch of Vedanta philosophy.
>    It asserts that *Brahman* (the Supreme Self, the
>    Absolute) alone exists, and that the world and the
>    individual self are illusory appearances within it.
>    Hence, *Advaitin*: one who follows the *Advaita*
>    philosophy.

Bhagavad Gita

>    An ancient philosophical and religious text
>    (literally: "The Song of the Blessed One") in which
>    the Hindu God Krishna tells Arjuna the warrior to
>    do his duty and fight a war without attachment to
>    its outcome.

*bhajans*

>    Songs of devotion.

*bhakta*

>    A devotee who follows the path of *bhakti*.

*bhakti*

>    Devotion as the path to salvation.

*brahmin*

>    In Hinduism, the priestly caste, or a member of this
>    caste, having the duties of learning, teaching, and
>    performing rites (*pujas*) and sacrifices (*yagnas*).

*dharma*

>    Inherent property or natural characteristic (e.g. the

*dharma* of fire is to burn). Also, a firm code of conduct and duty—the eternal principal of right action; moral duty; divine law; religious tradition.

*japa*

Repetition (usually after initiation), of a word or words (*mantra*) or a name of God; *japa* is a form of meditation which is practiced as a means of stilling the mind and invoking Grace or enlightenment.

*jnana*

Real and incontrovertible knowledge; the state in which one knows one's true nature experientially.

*jnani*

A sage; one who knows the Ultimate Reality.

*karma*

Action; the principle of causality; the impersonal mechanism by which manifestation and life as we know it functions. In Hinduism, *karma* is the law of retributive action which brings back upon the individual doer, in this or a future life, good or evil consequences for acts committed. Followers of the path of *karma* aim to reach enlightenment through selfless acts and deeds.

*kundalini*

Latent creative energy which lies coiled at the base of the spine; when aroused by spiritual practices, it rises up through the spine to the top of the head.

*leela*
> Spontaneous objectless play; especially applied to manifestation which is understood to be merely the Divine play of Consciousness or God.

*mala*
> In Hinduism, a rosary of 108 beads used in the practice of *japa*.

*mantra*
> A word or phrase given to a disciple by his guru; the repetition of a *mantra* (*mantra-japa*) is one of the most common forms of *sadhana*.

*maya*
> Literally a phantom image, an illusion; in Vedanta philosophy, it refers to the misconception whereby the ephemeral world of appearances if taken to be real.

*moksha*
> Spiritual liberation; enlightenment.

*nirvana*
> Spiritual liberation, through which ego-consciousness is completely "extinguished" or transcended.

*puja*
> The ceremonial worship of a Hindu deity.

*sadhana*
> Spiritual practice or method.

*samadhi*
> 1. The highest condition of human consciousness, in which the subject-object (seer-seen) distinction is transcended. 2. The memorial of a saint. 3. *Mahasamadhi*: the death of a saint.

*samsara*
> Worldly illusion; the cycle of birth and death.

*Sat-Chit-Ananda*
> Truth-Consciousness-Bliss.

*satsang*
> Association of the Truth; being in the presence of one who embodies the Ultimate Reality

*satguru*
> The guru within—the Self, or Consciousness; also, the transmitter of enlightenment.

*siddhis*
> Supernatural powers acquired through spiritual practices.

*yoga*
> Union; spiritual practice according to the philosophy of Patanjali.

**Enlightenment May Or May Not Happen** "The whole problem is that the individual seeks enlightenment as an object which can bring happiness, or the cessation of unhappiness. But so long as there is a 'me' seeking enlightenment, enlightenment cannot happen." This book, and its sequel **Enlightenment? Who Cares!**, document the teachings of Ramesh S. Balsekar, as expressed in response to questions regarding the spiritual search and related issues. In conversations recorded during his daily teaching sessions, Ramesh repeatedly affirms the impersonal nature of life and seeking. As the spiritual search progresses, the seeker's identification with the fictitious "me"-entity weakens until there is no one left to care whether enlightenment happens or not. "When you come to that stage, it is likely that enlightenment will happen at any time." A series of humorous cartoons accompany the transcripts, underscoring key aspects of the teachings they illustrate.

**Enlightenment by Airmail** and **Enlightenment à la Carte** Selected highlights of the lively and light-hearted cartoons which illustrate *Enlightenment May or May Not Happen* and *Enlightenment? Who Cares!* are gathered together into these two postcard collections. Each collection consists of a set of 20 detachable full-color cartoon postcards whose humor vividly highlights the wisdom of Ramesh's *Advaita* Vedanta teachings. Send them off to amuse and "enlighten" your relatives and friends!

Six First-Hand Accounts Of Enlightenment Occurences

**Enlightenment: An Outbreak**  In an absorbing series of interviews and intimate conversations, Ramesh S. Balsekar and five of his enlightened disciples describe their spiritual search and its culmination in enlightenment. The role of the guru in this process, and the nature of their post-enlightenment experience are explored. Full of fascinating insights and touching personal anecdotes, this book will appeal to anyone who is even remotely interested in spirituality.

**Teachings en Route to Freedom**

Throughout history, India has produced an extraordinary range of religious traditions and, even today, innumerable spiritual teachers can be found there. This book documents Madhukar Thompson's encounters with a wide range of gurus: Osho Rajneesh, U.G. Krishnamurti, Annamalai Swami, Ranjit Maharaj, Tulku Urgyen Rinpoche, Choekyi Nyima Rinpoche, Dadaji, Lakshmana Swami, Harish Madhukar, Andrew Cohen, Gangaji, Giridhar and Kiran whom he sought out in his quest for enlightenment. It presents a compilation of remarkably diverse spiritual teachings as expressed in conversations which were recorded over a period of 17 years.

**Of Jewels, Pigs and Freedom**  This is a selection of 14 full-color cartoons inspired by the teachings of Papaji (Sri Harilal Poonja), as featured in the book Enlightenment: Never Found – Never Lost. Devised by Madhukar Thompson who spent two years in Lucknow as one of Poonjaji's closest disciples, the clarity and humor of these postcards reflect the powerful experience of satsang with this remarkable guru.

**Zorba 'n Buddha Your Way to Freedom**  In this set of 14 full-color postcards, Madhukar Thompson takes a light-hearted, even mischievous, look at the world of Osho. His lengthy experience as one of Osho Rajneesh's disciples enables him to present an insider's view, pointing up the humorous aspects of a neo-sannyasin's life of celebration and meditation, and the controversial teachings of this notorious guru.

**Enlightenment: Never Found—Never Lost** This book documents the teachings of Papaji (Sri Harilal Poonja) using material drawn from extensive recordings of his *satsangs* held in Lucknow, India. Illustrated by a series of humorous cartoons devised by the editor, Madhukar Thompson, the book charts his experience as a disciple of Poonjaji. The dramatic "love affair" between the guru and the disciple eventually comes to an explosive end, but it also provides many precious insights into the guru-disciple relationship and the true nature of freedom.

*The Seeker and His Search*
*Meditation*
*Enlightenment*
*Master!*

Each of these postcard collections contains 10 detachable full-color cartoons devised by Madhukar Thompson. Their inspiration has been distilled from his experiences during two decades of spiritual search, and while each collection focuses on a different theme, their common purpose is to highlight the funny side of spirituality. They will be enjoyed by full-time, part-time (and even flexi-time!) seekers everywhere.

---

These titles may be ordered directly from Neti Neti Press or Pacifica. For further information, e-mail, write, call, or fax to:

**India**

Neti Neti Press
8 Sheetal Apts.
Kawedewadi
Koregaon Park
Pune  411001
Tel/Fax: 91-20-603338
or 6050020

**Germany**

Neti Neti Press
Kiefernweg 10
64319 Pfungstadt
Tel/Fax: 49-6157-3471
E-mail: (neti_neti@yahoo.com)
www.neti-neti.org

**USA**

Pacifica
P.O. Box 120
Haiku
Hawai, 96708
Tel: 1-888-740-1270
Fax: 1-808-575-2072
E-mail: mohanmaui@hotmail.com